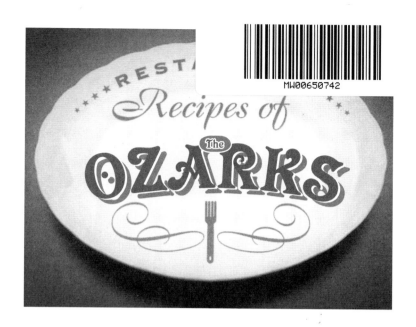

Compiled by
Restaurant Recipes

*You can now prepare and enjoy the colorful
tastes of the Missouri Ozarks in your own
kitchen. Featuring over 200 of the best
recipes from the area's favorite restaurants.*

Enjoy!

Special Thanks from the Editor:
This cookbook would not have been possible without the support of all the restaurant owners and chefs who appear in this book.

Copyright © 2006 Restaurant Recipes

Library of Congress Control Number: 2006903595

ISBN: 0-9778057-0-0

First Edition

Printed in China

Published by:
Restaurant Recipes
A division of Recipe Publishers
5225 W. 95th Street
Overland Park, KS 66207
(913) 271-9882

Editor: JE Cornwell
Senior Advisor: Judith A. Cornwell
Graphic Design: Tom Dease
Project Advisors: Jim & Ruth Martin

Contents

The Best of the Missouri Ozarks

4

★★★★★ RESTAURANT

Recipes of

APPETIZERS

4341 Beach Drive
Hwy. 54, Lake Road 22
17.5 Mile Marker on the Lake
Osage Beach, MO 65065
(573) 348-6639
www.bwjacks.com

Casual dining lakeside featuring south Florida cuisine with a Midwest flair, "Floribbean." Specials (excluding holidays), Mon - Ladies Night, Tues - Industry Night, Wed - Bikes, Blues & BBQ and Raw Deal Thursday - 99¢ Peel & Eat Shrimp, 65¢ Oysters on the 1/2 shell, & 35¢ Chicken Wings...Enjoy one of our famous Rum Runners anytime! Live music at the Tiki Bar. Kitchen, Lounge and open air deck open March - Nov: daily at 11 am.

Crab Cream-Cheese Stuffed Mushrooms

12 lbs. cream cheese
4 oz. chopped
2 oz. A1 sauce
2 c. Parmesan cheese

2½ lbs. red crab meat
2 oz. Worcestershire sauce
2 lbs. shredded cheddar
Silver dollar sized mushrooms

Directions

Mix ingredients in mixer. Stuff in silver dollar sized mushrooms. Bake in oven at 350° until cheese is golden brown on top. Sprinkle Parmesan cheese on top and serve.

Submitted by Backwater Jack's kitchen

401 N. Main
Laurie, MO 65038
(573) 374-6002

The Boardwalk Grill is a relaxed and casual seafood and steak house located in Laurie, Missouri. Steve and Nick Stock (owner/general manager) constructed the Boardwalk Grill in the spring of 2004. Operations began in early August of 2004. Open All Year at 11:00 a.m., Monday - Saturday. We hope that you enjoy a few of our favorite dishes!

Stuffed Mushrooms

1 lb. small mushrooms
5 Tbsp. green pepper
1 Tbsp. butter
1 tsp. salt
½ c. butter bread crumbs or cracker crumbs

4 slices bacon, cooked and diced
⅛ tsp. sugar
1 med. onion
2 (3 oz.) cream cheese, room temperature

Directions

Fry bacon until crisp. Remove bacon from drippings. Cook the remaining ingredients until tender (except cream cheese). Remove from heat and mix with cream cheese. Remove stems from mushrooms; chopped stems can be added to the cream cheese mixture. Stuff and mound the cream cheese mixture into each mushroom. Place in baking dish and add ¼ c. hot water. Spread the bread or cracker crumb mixture on top and bake for 20 minutes at 375°. Insert toothpicks.

Submitted by Nicholas Stock, general manager

CHEER'S BAR & GRILL

1212 Linn St
Sikeston, MO 63801
(573) 471-2006

Cheer's bar and grill began business in 1990 in a small 1500 sq. ft. building with approximately 4 employees. It has since grown into a 5000 sq. ft. building with 22 employees. We specialize in several areas. We have choice steaks, which are some of the best around. We also serve items not easily found in our area, such as cajun dishes, Mexican dishes, homemade burgers, tamales and a variety of fish and seafood. All our food is homemade! We also have a full bar. Come by and see our lake and the ducks our back of our sunroom. It's beautiful and makes for romantic dining.

German Fries

2 baked potatoes
Salt
¼ c. chopped onion

2 strips bacon
Pepper

Directions

Cut hearts out of baked potatoes and put in a pan with 1 Tbsp. of butter. Add crumbled bacon, salt and pepper to taste and ¼ c. chopped onions. Saute until browned. These are excellent. Can substitute green onions if preferred.

Fried Green Tomatoes

2 green tomatoes
Salt
1 egg

Flour
Pepper
1 c. milk

Directions

Make egg wash with 1 egg and 1 c. milk. Beat egg into milk. Cut 2 green tomatoes into slices. Bread tomatoes with flour and then dip in milk and egg batter and again in flour an deep fry until golden brown.

Submitted by Joyce Winchester, owner

8

CLASSIC SPORTS CAFE

Inside the Clarion Hotel
3333 S. Glenstone
Springfield, MO 65804
417-883-6550

Classic's Sports Café located in the Clarion Hotel is one of Springfield's Best Sports Bar & Grille. Offering over 20 TV's, you will have no problem finding your favorite game. A great menu featuring appetizers, sandwiches, steaks and our Award Winning Barbecue. The fun, casual atmosphere provides a great setting for Alumni Watch Parties, Social Clubs and Birthday Parties.

Major League Wings

½ c. cayenne pepper hot sauce
1 tsp. Tobasco
½ tsp. garlic

½ c. tomato sauce
1 tsp. red pepper flakes
Chicken wings

Directions

Combine all ingredients except chicken. Deep fry or bake chicken wings until done. Toss cooked wings in sauce. Serve with celery sticks and blue cheese or ranch dressing.

Submitted by Chef John Blansit

CLUB 60 STEAKHOUSE

8773 Old Hwy. 60
Mountain Grove, MO 65711
(417) 926-9954

The Club 60 Steakhouse and saloon has been around for many years, but just recently acquired new owners Jim and Robin Alessi, transplanted from NY. Mostly known for their great chargrilled steaks, they also feature hand breaded pork tenderloin, chicken fried steak and chicken fingers, seafood and Italian fare.

Roasted Garlic Parmesan Homefries

8-10 Idaho or large red potatoes
4 Tbsp. olive oil
4 Tbsp. grated Parmesan cheese

4 Tbsp. minced garlic
Salt and pepper

Directions

Boil potatoes until they are fork tender in the middle (Approx. 20 minutes). Drain water and cool for 3-4 hours. Preheat oven to 350°. Cube potatoes leaving skin on. Stir in olive oil, minced garlic and salt and pepper to taste. For a twist, use garlic pepper, lemon pepper, cajun or Caribbean jerk spice. Spread evenly onto a sheet pan and sprinkle with Parmesan cheese. Place in oven for approx. 10 minutes or until golden brown and crispy, stirring after 5 minutes to prevent sticking.

Submitted by Robin Alessi

10

CLUB 609

609 S. Main St.
Joplin, MO 64801
(417) 623-6090

The following recipe is a favorite in our town—if not enjoyed many other ways, in many other restaurants. This is the "Club 609 version", best served with sour cream, and a favorite salsa—be sure to get the dip, sour cream, and salsa on the chip for the perfect bite!

Spinach and Artichoke Dip

2 packages (approx. 14 oz. each) frozen chopped spinach
½ c. - 1 c. artichoke hearts
2 Tbsp. garlic powder
Shredded Mozzerella

1 c. mayonnaise
½ c. shredded Parmesan
Tortilla chips

Directions

Preheat oven to 350°.

Thaw the spinach, then squeeze out any excess water. Drain the artichokes as well, and zip them through the food processor. Place the spinach, artichokes, mayonnaise, garlic powder and Parmesan in a large bowl and mix thoroughly. If the mixture is a little dry, add more mayonnaise. It should be moist. Place the mixture in a baking dish, and top with mozzarella, covering the dip completely. Bake for about 25 minutes or until the cheese is brown on top. Serve immediately with tortilla chips, sour cream and salsa.

Submitted by Linda Shepard, owner, and Meg Shelfer, kitchen manager

DOWD'S CATFISH & BBQ

I'M HOOKED ON
DOWD'S CATFISH AND B·B·Q
LEBANON, MO

1760 W. Elm
Lebanon, MO 65536
(417) 532-1777

This is our version of shrimp scampi with a creamy garlic sauce. One of our customers favorites, along with our award winning catfish and tasty Bar-B-Q. We have a full menu. Come on in and find your favorite!

Shrimp Scampi

1 clove garlic, chopped
3 strips yellow bell pepper
6 strips green bell pepper
3 strips red bell pepper
(bell peppers to be cut into ¼ wide strips)
¼ med. onion, cut in wedges
½ tsp. garlic salt
1 c. heavy whipping cream
½ tsp. granulated garlic
3 lemon wedges
½ stick butter
10 pieces peeled & deveined shrimp
(21-25 count)
7 oz. linguini, precooked
Parsley flakes

Directions

Saute onions, peppers and garlic in butter until tender (about 3 min. - do not over cook)! Add shrimp, continue to Saute until shrimp is no longer clear looking (about 3 min.). Add spices, heavy whipping cream and pasta. Continue sauteing about 2 minutes. Serve in large bowl or large deep dish. Garnish with lemon wedges and chopped parsley flakes.

Submitted by Gary Dyer, owner

GARBO'S PIZZERIA

Garbo's Pizzeria Midtown
307 S. National
Springfield, MO 65802
(417) 831-9010

Garbo's Pizzeria Chesterfield Village
2101 W. Chesterfield Blvd.
Springfield, MO 65807
(417) 883-9010

The "Pesto Pie" was created as an appetizer or entree for a single person dining alone and also to fit the vegetarian slot–although it does not qualify as vegan. We use real dairy at Garbo's. This appetizer goes well alone or with our Garbo's Salads. Come on in and we will be glad to hook you up. We are a full-service restaurant with a full bar.

Pesto Pie

1 - 10" Mama Lupés Flour Tortilla Shell
3 Tbsp. Classic Pesto Sauce
2 large mushrooms
¼ c. provel

1 tsp. ground oregano
1 med. red onion
¼ c. Mozzarella

Optional ingredients: green peppers, black olives, jalapenos (nice additions)

Directions

Slice your medium red onion as thin as you can. Cut and dice up your mushrooms. With a large spoon evenly spread your pesto sauce to ¼" from the edges of burrito shell. Sprinkle your mushrooms over your shell lightly, then proceed to do the same with your red onions and any optional ingredients. Mix your mozzarella and provel together in a small bowl then sprinkle over all ingredients on shell to ¼" from edges. Last but not least–a light shake of oregano.

Preheat oven to 500°. Put shell on stone or a pizza pan with holes. Cook 10-12 minutes until bubbly or melted to your liking.

Submitted by Pam Babcock, owner

**211 W. Battlefield
Springfield, MO 65807
(417) 881-9558**

Gem of India has been serving Springfield with fine Indian cuisine for the past 3 years. The chef/owner has worked in fine Indian restaurants in Boston since 1992. We serve authentic Indian cuisine made with the finest and freshest ingredients. We strive to provide excellent service and mouth watering delicacies with enticing ambience. We hope to serve Springfield for a long time to come.

Chicken Curry Dip

2 Tbsp. olive oil
1 tsp. chili flakes
1 tsp. turmeric
1 chicken breast, diced
2 tomatoes, diced
1 lime, juiced
2 tortillas, toasted

1 tsp. chili powder
2 garlic cloves, peeled and crushed
1 tsp. ginger
½ onion, peeled and diced
110 ml/4 fl. oz. double cream
3 Tbsp. fresh coriander, chopped

Directions

Preheat a medium pan. Heat the oil in the pan before adding the spices and frying for 2 minutes. Add the chicken and sauté for 2 minutes. Add the onion and tomatoes and leave curry to simmer for 6 minutes. Pour in the cream and add the lime juice. When the cream has heated through and reduced, remove the curry from the heat. Add the coriander and stir well. Transfer the curry to a large deep bowl and serve with toasted tortilla.

Submitted by Gurdev Singh, owner

HICKOK'S STEAKHOUSE & BREWERY

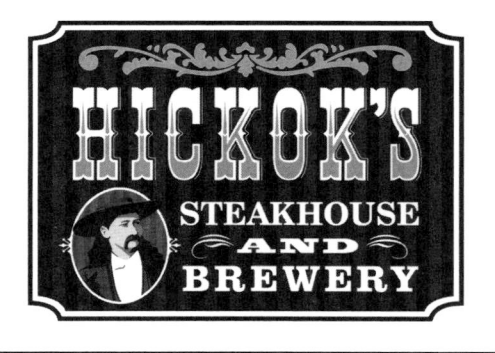

314 S. Patton
Springfield, MO 65804
(417) 872-1141
www.hickokssteakhouse.com

Family friendly, fun, and Affordable. The newest steakhouse in town. Hickok's Steakhouse and Brewery. Come visit the old west in one of the oldest buildings in downtown Springfield only a block from where the famous gunfight between Wild Bill Hickok and Dave Tutt happened in 1865. The first fast draw gunfight in America. Great Food, Great Beer, Great Fun, Lunch or Dinner Monday through Saturday. All at a Great Price. Hickok's Steakhouse and Brewery.

Chorizo Stuffed Portabella Caps

A sturdy appetizer that can be a meal in itself.
Best served with a pint of handcrafted Copperhead Ale.

1½ lbs. hot chorizo
1 c. seasoned bread crumbs
¾ tsp. black pepper
1 Tbsp. butter, melted
½ c. chicken stock
½ tsp. cayenne pepper

6 eggs, beaten
1½ tsp. fresh sage, chopped
1 pinch nutmeg
3 c. stale biscuits
½ Tbsp. salt

Directions

Stuffing: Brown off sausage. Set aside to cool. Beat eggs and add bread crumbs, butter and seasonings. Add sausage and biscuits. Mix well and bake in a casserole dish for 15-20 minutes at 350°. Let cool.

Mushrooms: Remove stems and gills from cap using a spoon. Rub cap with oil, salt and pepper and cook until almost done. Allow to cool, then stuff. Refrigerate until needed. Reheat at 400° until stuffing reaches internal temperature of 140°. Serve plated and drizzled with queso.

Submitted by Kevin Sparks, chef de cuisine

Other Books From The Publisher

The Menu Guide of Kansas City

Restaurant Recipes of Kansas City

The Kansas City Chiefs Cookbook

To Order Call:

(913) 271-9882

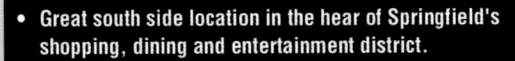

1252 Hwy. KK
Osage Beach, MO 65065
(573) 348-1735

Mitch & Duff's at Dogwood Hills is named after two of the owners who have also served as golf pros for Dogwood Hills Golf Club. When the clubhouse was remodeled and expanded to accommodate the restaurant, many names were suggested for the new facility, but it finally came down to this simple and descriptive name.

White Cheese Dip

½ lb. white Cheddar cheese   ½ lb. Munster cheese
½ lb. Monterrey Jack cheese   12 oz. jar processed white cheese spread
6 oz. can or Rotel (hot, medium or mild) to taste

Directions

Cube all cheese and combine cheese spread and Rotel. Melt all ingredients in a double boiler or microwave stirring frequently until smooth. Serve with your favorite chips or crackers (celery is good too for those carb watchers). This is a cheese sauce that can be used as a topping for many dishes or in other recipes.

Submitted by Ron Schlicht, general manager

SKYBOX GRILLE & LOUNGE

1271 East Montclair
Springfield, MO 65804
(417) 877-9595

Skybox is Southwest Missouri's best sports bar and grille. It features more than 20 TVs throughout . With the state of the art kitchen headed up by Chef Robert McLing, Skybox provides different daily lunch specials, along with its main menu that has something for everyone. An outdoor patio, a v.i.p. room and newly added game room provide Skybox customers a great experience every time. Skybox can also handle all your catering needs as well as large or small group parties.

Spinach Artichoke Dip

A hearty favorite with three varieties of cheese and real heavy cream. It pairs well with tortilla chips or wedges of fococcia bread.

1½ c. heavy cream	6 oz. minced yellow onion
8 oz. shredded Mozzarella	1 tsp. Tabasco sauce
8 oz. softened cream cheese	8 oz. grated Parmesan cheese
2 Tbsp. minced garlic	1 oz. olive oil
1 Tbsp. Worcestershire sauce	Salt, white pepper to taste
1 lb. chopped fresh spinach	Fococcia bread - wedged
2 16-oz. cans chopped artichokes	Tortilla chips

Directions

Heat olive oil in a sauce pan. Add onions and garlic, sauté until onions are translucent. Add heavy cream, bring to a simmer, add cream cheese and stir until melted. Add Worcestershire sauce and Tabasco, then spinach and artichokes. Cook for 10 minutes at a simmer, then add the remaining cheeses, stirring to incorporate well. Serve in a bowl topped with a little Parmesan and tortilla chips and Fococcia on the side.

Submitted by Robert F. McLing, chef-manager

SPORTS BAR & GRILL

107 3rd Street
Monett, MO 65708
(417) 236-9500
www.shortstopbarrocks.com

Sports Bar & Grill originated in February 2004. There, you can find a very friendly atmosphere and great food. The menu boasts anything from the best burger in town to a mouth-watering steak. Prime rib is available on weekends, too! Sports Bar & Grill also has a full bar. We have many favorites on our menu including the following recipe.

Blackened Chicken Quesadilla

7 oz. chicken breast
Tortilla shell, flavored
Black beans

Blackened redfish seasoning
Cheddar cheese, grated
Butter, melted

Directions

Press chicken into seasoning on both sides. Pour butter onto flat grill, place chicken on grill. Pour butter over chicken periodically while it is cooking. Pour more butter onto grill and place tortilla shell on top of butter. Make sure there is butter under the whole tortilla. Spread cheese over whole tortilla, sprinkle beans on half. When chicken is cooked, chop into small pieces and spread over half. When cheese is melted and tortilla shell is crisp, fold in half. Cut into serving slices and serve with shredded lettuce, black olives, chopped tomatoes and jalapeno slices. On the side we offer sour cream, guacamole, salsa or our own homemade pico de gallo. We would love to give you the recipe for our pico de gallo, but you will just have to come here and try it.

Submitted by Lois Phillips

WellspringCafe

Delicious Homemade Vegetarian Foods
Daily Specials ~ Finest Natural Ingredients

300 W. McDaniel
Springfield, MO 65806
(417) 865-1818

Wellspring Cafe is a family-owned vegan restaurant located in beautiful, downtown Springfield, Mo. All of our recipes have been developed without using eggs or dairy products and feature an ever-increasing variety of organic and locally produced foods. Most of our menu, our breads and baked treats are from recipes developed over the past 25 years using whole grains and alternative sweeteners. Join us for lunch Monday through Friday from 11 a.m. to 3 p.m.

Avocado Pico de Gallo

1 diced avocado
⅔ c. diced fresh tomato
⅓ c. diced fresh red onion
2 Tbsp. minced fresh garlic

¼ c. fresh lime juice
¼ c. chopped fresh cilantro
1 Tbsp. minced fresh jalapeno
½ tsp. salt

Directions

Mix all the ingredients together. Garnish with sprigs of fresh cilantro and serve as a dip with tortilla chips or as a side with your favorite Spanish dish. For a variation, add 1 cup of cooked drained black beans.

Submitted by Paul and Nancy Day, owners

WHITE RIVER FISH COMPANY

Located at Bass Pro Shops
The Branson Landing
Branson, Missouri
COMING SOON

The 11,255 sq. ft. floating White River Fish Company restaurant is part of the all new Bass Pro Shops retail store in Branson, MO. Located at the Branson Landing development adjacent to historic downtown and Lake Taneycomo. In addition to the floating restaurant other features of the Branson location will include an approximate 68-slip operating marina, guide service, boat rental and boat service center. The Bass Pro Shops store is tentatively scheduled to open in June.

Southwestern Shrimp Dip

½ lb. Precooked shrimp, thawed and pureed
½ c. heavy mayonnaise
½ small red onion, chopped very fine
¼ tsp. Tabasco
¼ tsp. granulated garlic
Pepper to taste

½ lb. cream cheese
½ small red pepper, chopped very fine
½ oz. jalapeno, chopped
1 Tbsp. key lime juice
Salt to taste
1 tsp. dried chives

Soften cream cheese. Add all ingredients in a mixer. Mix well. Makes 1½ lbs.

Blue Crab Dip

½ lb. blue crab meat (stone crab also works)
¼ c. heavy mayonnaise
¼ tsp. horseradish
Salt and pepper to taste

½ lb. cream cheese
1 tsp. dried chives
3 drops Tabasco

Soften cream cheese. Add all ingredients in a mixer. Mix well. Makes 1½ lbs.

Submitted by Steven Todd, general manager

612 Devil's Pool Road
Ridgedale, MO 65739
(417) 335-2777

A former country retreat for Frisco Railroad executive Harry Worman, this elegant setting is home to our elaborate Champagne Sunday Brunch. No effort is spared to bring you the finest in culinary offerings amid luxurious surroundings. Our Sunday brunch features fresh fruits and breakfast breads, salads and charcuterie, delicious hot entrees, omelettes cooked to order and Belgian waffles, freshly carved meats and delectable desserts. Some traditional favorites are served weekly, while our chefs prepare a variety of special offerings each Sunday.

Chesapeake Crab Trio

Crab Cake

1 green bell pepper, diced
½ Tbsp. old bay seasoning
1 c. mayonnaise
2 c. bread crumbs

½ red onion, diced
½ Tbsp. Dijon mustard
1 lb. lump crabmeat

Mix all ingredients together except crab and bread crumbs. Fold in crab meat just to blend, add bread crumbs and fold into 2 oz. cakes, coat with flour and sauté.

Crab Imperial

½ lb. crab meat
1 Tbsp Dijon mustard
1 c. mayonnaise
2 ea. Roma tomatoes, diced

½ Tbsp. old bay seasoning
1 egg
½ Tbsp. fresh tarragon, chopped

Mix all ingredients in large bowl except crab. Then fold in crab meat.

Crab Norfolk

1½ lb. crab meat
½ Tbsp. butter, softened
½ oz. white wine

⅛ tsp. dill
⅛ tsp. bacon bits

Mix all ingredients of Crab Norfolk together. Pan sear crab cake. Sautée crab Norfolk. Bake Crab Imperial in a 500° oven for 4 minutes. Serve all on one plate.

Submitted by Todd Leonard, asst. food and beverage director

1622 Horseshoe Bend Pkwy.
P.O. Box 1547
Lake Ozark, MO 65049
(573) 365-2800

Andre's Restaurant - an inviting restaurant situated atop a bluff overlooking The Lake of the Ozarks, provides diners a change from the Ordinary. It is located on Horseshoebend Parkway, close to resorts and hotels The owner Andre Torres, a certified executive chef, oversees the daily operation. Andre's food transports diners around a world of culinary delights-steaks grilled on a woodfire grill, lobster with a champagne butter, chicken, fish, veal, and pasta. Inside Andre's, make sure you have a martini at Le Fou Bar - (a great bar with a vast martini list, specialty drinks, and a light bar menu) During summer do not miss Sunday Brunch from 9:00AM-1:00PM. Cooking classes September to May at 6:00 PM International night every third Friday of the Month.

Goat Cheese Pillow in Herbed Tomato Broth

3 sheets phyllo dough (cut into quarters)
Mix the following:

¼ c. clarified butter	4 oz. goat cheese
1 Tbsp. chives, chopped	1 tsp. garlic, chopped
Salt and pepper	

Tomato Broth:

1 c. tomato juice	1 tsp. garlic, chopped
¼ tsp. thyme	Spring rosemary
1 tsp. peppercorns, cracked	Pinch anise seeds
Salt and pepper	1 Tbsp. cornstarch, enough to thicken

Directions

Put all ingredients in a small pot and bring to a boil. Reduce heat to a simmer and let simmer for 5 minutes. Strain and thicken. Butter phyllo dough and put goat cheese in the center of dough. Cover it with butter. Bake at 350° for 4-5 minutes.

Put broth on the plate and then goat cheese pillow on top and serve.

Submitted Andre Torres, owner and executive chef

AVANZARE ITALIAN DINING

S.E. corner of Glenstone
& Sunshine
1908 S. Glenstone
Springfield, MO
(417) 567-3463
www.avanzareitaliandining.com

Exceptional Northern Italian cuisine is the center piece of Avanzare. As you dine with us, you'll find world class chef Tony Garcia prepares each dish with only the finest freshly sourced ingredients, including fresh made bread and desserts. A little bit of Italy sits quietly On The Plaza at Glenstone and Sunshine. Surrounding ourselves with only the best ensures your dining experience at Avanzare is what you anticipate and deserve!

La Torre di Pisa Caprese

Local vine-ripened tomatoes that are firm, red, juicy & flavorful, preferably unrefrigerated

Truly fragrant, flavorful young basil: green basil grown in the earth & sun-quality fresh, moist mozzarella 'mozzarella di bufala' from Naples region
    substitute: good fresh cow's milk mozzarella (called Fior di latte)

Genuine extra-virgin olive oil - (only olive oil and make it the best you can afford!)

Balsamic vinaigrette - this must be a quality blend

Kalamata Olives

Directions

Slice the fresh mozzarella into discs of moderate thickness.
Slice the discs of the ripe tomatoes.
Tear a good bunch of fresh basil leaves.
Add salt & freshly ground pepper to taste.

Begin building your Tower:
Layer the tomatoes & mozzarella - begin with a firm slice of tomato.
Place basil leaves as desired.
Garnish plate with olives.

Drizzle Balsamic vinaigrette & Olive Oil on and around your tower
Toasted Baguette bread would compliment the flavors of your salad.

Submitted by Avanzare Staff

BALDKNOBBERS COUNTRY RESTAURANT

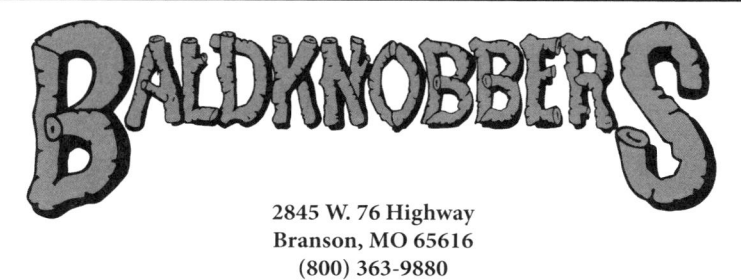

2845 W. 76 Highway
Branson, MO 65616
(800) 363-9880
(417) 335-6664

Baldknobbers Country Restaurant – Take a break from the food chains and enjoy home style cooking with a full menu plus breakfast (7 a.m. to 11 a.m.), lunch (11 a.m. to 4 p.m.) and dinner (4 p.m. to close) buffets. All served with an Ozarks flavor in a warm welcome country atmosphere. Open daily. Next to the Baldknobbers Jamboree Theatre.

Taco Salad

1 lb. hamburger
½ c. sour cream
Dash lemon juice
1 bag shredded cheddar cheese
1½ c. taco sauce
1 medium tomato, chopped

1 envelope taco seasoning
1 avocado
8 oz. cream cheese
¾ c. water
1 small onion, chopped
1 head lettuce (in bite-sized pieces)

Directions

Brown meat and drain. Add taco seasoning and water and cook 15 minutes. Place lettuce on serving plates. Top with onion, tomato and cheese. Crumble chips n top. Pour hamburger and juice over top. Pour avocado mixture over meat and top with taco sauce. Garnish with halved black olives. Serves 6.

Submitted by Baldknobbers Staff

CANDLESTICK INN

127 Taney Street
Branson, MO 66616
(417) 334-3633

Pumpkin Soup with Cinnamon Croutons

This is a great Fall soup for those cold days. It is also great around the holidays.

Soup:

1 qt. heavy cream
¼ c. honey
½ c. maple syrup
1 pinch of cloves/ground

1 c. canned pumpkin
½ c. brown sugar
1 pinch cinnamon

Croutons:

5 pieces white bread
1 Tbsp. maple syrup
1 pinch cinnamon

1 Tbsp. brown sugar
1 Tbsp. butter

Directions

Soup: Bring all ingredients to a boil over medium heat. Simmer until right consistency (soup thickness).

Croutons: Melt butter and mix with other ingredients. Toss cut bread in mixture and bake in 350° oven until crisp (about 10 minutes).

Submitted by Jason Watson, chef

CLUB 60 STEAKHOUSE

8773 Old Hwy. 60
Mountain Grove, MO 65711
(417) 926-9954

Owner, Jim Alessi is well known for his delicious homemade soups. So much so that most of his regular customers order the soup and then ask what kind it is. This recipe is a club 60 favorite. Our customers love to dip our homemade bread in this hearty soup that eats like a meal.

Club 60 Beef Barley Soup

1 med. onion, diced
4 med. tomatoes, diced
1 green pepper, diced
1 lb. spinach, chopped
1 can tomato (10-12 oz.)
5 Tbsp. olive oil
2 sirloin steaks, cubed (12 oz. raw)

5 cloves garlic, chopped
6 med. carrots, diced
1 stalk celery, diced
2 cans beef broth (10-12 oz.)
1 box of barley (12-16 oz.)
8 Tbsp. butter

Directions

In a large saucepan, add barley and fill with water approx. 3 inches above barley. Add a pinch of salt. Bring to a boil for 5 minutes. Turn off heat and set aside.

In a large stock pot, sautee onions, peppers, garlic, tomatoes and a pinch of salt and pepper in butter and 3 Tbsp. olive oil over med-low heat for about 5 minutes. (for added flavor, use garlic pepper or lemon pepper or a combination of both) Fill the pot ⅓ with water and add carrots and celery. Sprinkle steak with a pinch of salt, pepper and remaining 2 Tbsp. olive oil. Stir in steak, spinach, tomato sauce and beef broth. Rinse barley in a strainer with cold water and add to pot. Simmer on med-high heat for 20- 30 minutes and serve.

Submitted by Robin Alessi

EMACK & BOLIO'S

216 E. Walnut St
Springfield, MO 65806
(417) 831-6336
www.emacksdowntown.com

Award-winning Boston ice cream. Smoothies, coffee, espresso, homemade soups, sandwiches and salads. All breads, pastries, and desserts are made from scratch. Fresh squeezed juices and smoothies come with vitamins, power boosters and energy shots while the cold creamy stuff comes in funky flavors like Grasshopper Pie and Twisted Dee-Light.

Emack & Bolio's Cream of Mushroom Soup

2 Tbsp. olive oil
1 small white onion, chopped
1 Tbsp. dried thyme
1 qt. heavy whipping cream
Salt

2 Tbsp. unsalted butter
2 lb. button mushrooms, chopped
½ c. all-purpose flour
2 qts. chicken broth
White pepper, freshly ground

Directions

Heat olive oil and butter over medium heat in a 5 quart stock pot. Add onion. Cook until onion begins to soften. Stir in mushrooms and cook until soft. Stir constantly and add flour and cook for 2 minutes. Gradually whisk in the broth. Add the thyme and bring to a simmer. Cook for 30 minutes. Add the heavy cream and season with salt and pepper to taste. Heat the soup but do not let it boil

Submitted by Debbie Bingham, owner

FLAME STEAKHOUSE & WINE BAR

314 W. Walnut St.
Springfield, MO 65806
(417) 862-4444

Flame Steakhouse & Wine Bar has been open for one year. The menu consists of four different aged steaks. In the lounge, which is known as the "Red Room," there is a glass room where guests can see the steaks aging. Decor is very eclectic, incredible service and a wine list.

Garbage Salad

Romaine & iceberg lettuce
Oven dried tomatoes
Applewood smoked bacon
Grilled steak

Cucumbers
Blue cheese crumbles
Spiced pecans

Directions

Combine all ingredients and serve with a good Italian vinaigrette, blue cheese or ranch dressing

Submitted by Mike Jalili, owner

Grace Cafe

818 Broadway
Cape Girardeau, MO 63701
(573) 334-2448

Grace Cafe is located near Southeast Missouri State University. Walk in to the aroma of freshly brewed coffee in an informal coffeehouse setting that has high speed WiFi and LAN internet connections. Friday nights feature talented musicians. Visit our website: www.capegracecafe.com

St. Francis Soup

¾ c. olive oil
12 c. vegan broth

16 garlic cloves, minced
1 c. ea. leaks, zucchini, artichoke hearts, chopped

Directions

Sauté garlic in oil Add broth. Add vegetables and simmer for one hour.

Girardot Greens

Mixed spring greens
¼ c. crumbled feta cheese
¼ c. dried cranberries

1 Tbsp. sunflower seeds
2 oz. raspberry vinaigrette

Directions

Place serving of greens on plate. Top with ¼ c. feta cheese and then cranberries. Serve with sunflower seeds and dressing.

Submitted by Grace Parry

913 Preacher Roe Blvd.
West Plain, MO 65775
(417) 257-9151
www.grapevinecafe.biz

Grapevine Wine Shop and Café offers a totally original dining and shopping experience with a unique combination of a full-service restaurant combined with a wine and gift shop. Lunch and dinner guests have the unusual option of buying wine at retail prices from the store, and drinking it with their meal with no additional charges. Grapevine features a wide variety of items ranging from grilled sandwiches to classic Italian dishes and offers the area's most extensive selection of wines, top shelf liquors, and specialty beers in a fun and eclectic atmosphere.

Grapevine Chicken Salad

1 lb. boneless, skinless chicken breasts
   (about 4 half breasts)
1 c. red seedless grades
½ c. pecan pieces
1 tsp. Dijon mustard

1 20-oz. chunk pineapple, well drained
1 med. red delicious, diced
½ c. celery, diced
½ c. mayonnaise

Directions

Lightly season chicken with salt and pepper and a sprinkle of Italian seasoning mix. Cook in 350° oven for 12 to 15 minutes. Don't over cook. Remove from oven and cool completely before adding the rest of ingredients. When chicken is completely cool, dice into ¼-in. pieces.

Completely drain pineapple, dice apple pieces about the size of the grapes and pineapple chunks. Dice celery. Place all ingredients into a large bowl and mix gently but thoroughly with large spoon or spatula. Place into container, cover and cool in refrigerator. Cool for at least one hour. Use within 4 days.

Submitted by Toni Chritton-Johnson, owner

HART'S CATFISH

3933 S. Westwood Blvd.
Poplar Bluff, MO 63901
(573) 686-2602

Hart's Catfish has been serving fresh, pond raised channel catfish for 17 years. We have served folks from nearly every state and several foreign countries. We're just a down-home place. To make our food heart healthy, we use only Rice Bran oil for deep frying and in our recipes. It contains no trans-fats and is 100% cholesterol free. A plate of our golden brown catfish served with our homemade hush puppies and tangy slaw is a favorite of many of our customers.

Sweet & Sour Slaw

1 head cabbage
1 c. sugar
1 tsp. black pepper
1 c. white vinegar
Optional ingredients:
1 onion, chopped
1 tsp. celery seed

1 carrot
1 tsp. salt
1Tbsp. prepared mustard
¼ c. rice bran oil

1 green pepper, chopped

Directions

Shred cabbage. Add grated carrot. Mix together sugar, salt, pepper, mustard and vinegar. Add rice oil. Pour over cabbage mix and stir (cabbage will wilt down). Be sure you have plenty of dressing on cabbage. Marinate over night. Store in glass jars in refrigerator. Keeps well.

Submitted by Sally Hart, manager

PAIRINGS RESTAURANT

Hwy. 160 & AA
381 W. Guin Road
Nixa, MO 65714
(417) 725-1998

Nixa's first fine dining restaurant brings a "DISCOVERY MENU" concept to SW Missouri. The Flynns transformed their 1979 Frank Lloyd Wright inspired structure, restoring it back to its original character, creating a cozy, metropolitan feel within a casual relaxed, and rustic atmosphere. The objective of Pairings Restaurant is to introduce its customers to the magic that can be created when specific foods are matched with a perfectly balanced wine. Chef Scott Myers has specially created & prepared each food item to pair with a specific wine. He adjusts the ingredients, herbs, and spices to bring out the flavors of the wine & the food when they are enjoyed together. He uses only the finest & freshest ingredients available. The restaurant also serves as a premier location for weddings, receptions, private business luncheons and parties with its beautifully landscaped setting overlooking the river.

Indoor and outdoor seating for up to 200 guests.

Organic Baby Bibb Salad
with a buttermilk and tarragon vinaigrette and house made croutons

1 head of baby bibb lettuce
1 c. buttermilk
½ shallot, minced
Salt to taste
½ c. blended olive oil
Croutons:
1 baguette with crust trimmed off and
    cut into ¼" cubes
¼ tsp. dried parsley
¼ c. olive oil

2 Tbsp. chopped fresh tarragon
1 clove garlic, minced
⅛ c. rice wine vinegar
White pepper to taste

½ tsp. dried basil
½ tsp. dried oregano
¼ tsp. garlic powder

Directions

For the vinaigrette: Add garlic, shallot and tarragon to buttermilk and steep at room temperature for 30 minutes. Slowly whisk in vinegar and then drizzle in oil to from an emulsion. Season with salt and white pepper to taste and reserve.

For croutons: Remove crust from baguette and cut into ¼" cubes. Toss in oil, dried herbs and garlic powder and season with salt and bake in oven until golden brown and crisp at 350°.

Recipe continued on next page

Organic Baby Bibb Salad...continued

For bibb lettuce: Remove outside leaves if bruised and trim the bottom stalk just to remove the brown color on the stem but making sure to keep the head of lettuce whole. Submerge in lukewarm water to remove any sand or dirt from the lettuce. Flip upside down and place on a wire rack to drip dry.

To assemble: Add 2 oz. of vinaigrette to a bowl and places the bibb lettuce in the bowl. Season with a touch of salt and pepper if desired toss and plate. Sprinkle with about 5 to 6 croutons and garnish with baby micro greens, edible flowers or your favorite cheese.

Spring Garlic Soup with Tiny Garlic Shoots

10 cloves and stalks of spring garlic	3 c. milk
2 med. yukon gold potatoes, small dice	½ shallot, minced
2 c. heavy cream	½ c. vegetable stock
4 garlic shoots per bowl	Salt and pepper to taste
4 oz. chives	½ c. olive oil

Directions

For the chive oil: Add chives in blender and start the motor and slowly drizzle oil in. If you need to add a bit more oil do so just to make the chive puree nice and smooth. Puree for 3 minutes and strain slowly through a fine mesh strainer.

For soup: Cut the garlic into smaller pieces (into thirds) Poach in 1½ cups of the milk for 30 seconds and then strain. Take the second 1.5 cups of milk bring to a simmer and place the garlic in the milk and poach again for 30 seconds. Strain garlic, discard the milk and reserve.

In a sauce pot heat 1 Tbsp. of olive oil and a Tbsp. of butter and add shallots. Turn heat down to low and sweat shallots for 2 minutes until they turn translucent. Add small dice yukon golds, garlic, veg stock and cream and bring up to a rolling simmer.

Simmer for about 20 minutes or until potatoes are cooked through. Place soup in a blender and start on low and increase it to high and puree for three minutes. Strain through a fine mesh strainer into another sauce pot. Bring soup back up to temperature and season to taste.

Ladel 4 oz. into a bowl of your choice and garnish with garlic shoots and chive oil.

Submitted by Chef Scott Myers

SCALLIONS

OTC's student operated upscale restaurant

Located at Ozarks Technical Community College
Info Commons Building, West End
1001 E. Chestnut Expwy. • Springfield, MO 65806
(417) 447-8283

Scallions is the student operated upscale eatery located on the campus of Ozarks Technical Community College in the Information Commons West building. Scallions opened it's doors to the public in 2001 as a method for upper level students to have the opportunity to work in a real world restaurant setting learning all aspects of the restaurant from front to the back. The Scallions menu and logo changes every semester to reflect changing food trends and to allow students to experience a wide range of culture and cuisines. From Greek to Mexican to a taste of Georgia each semester provides a menu that is unique and special. Scallions is open to the general public and walk in are welcome but reservations are definitely recommended.

Corn Crusted Lobster Salad
with Vanilla Vinaigrette

Batter:
2 c. flour
½ tsp. baking powder
½ c. roasted corn (pureed)
1½ c. club soda
1 tsp. vanilla extract
Pinch of salt

Vinegar Vanilla:
½ c. rice wine vinegar
1 c. salad oil
1 tsp. pepper
1 tsp. vanilla extract
1 tsp. salt
2 Tbsp. honey

Mix all ingredients except oil. Add oil slowly. Whisk until emulsified.

Salad:
12 oz. lobster meat
2 oz. zucchini/yellow squash (julienne)
4 sliced red onion
12 oz. meschu green
2 oz. carrot (julienne)
8 wedges tomato

1 tortilla wrap, shredded then fried crisp or baked

Directions

Mix all batter ingredients. Whisk until smooth. Coat lobster with batter and deep fry until golden brown. Place greens in center of bowl. Fan chipotle tortilla wedges onone side. Scatter veggies and lobster onto greens. Lay on the tomato, red onion and tortilla shreds. Drizzle with the dressing and serve.

Submitted by Chef Lou Rice

SCALLIONS

OTC's student operated upscale restaurant

Located at Ozarks Technical Community College
Info Commons Building, West End
1001 E. Chestnut Expwy. • Springfield, MO 65806
(417) 447-8283

Scallions is the student operated upscale eatery located on the campus of Ozarks Technical Community College in the Information Commons West building. Scallions opened it's doors to the public in 2001 as a method for upper level students to have the opportunity to work in a real world restaurant setting learning all aspects of the restaurant from front to the back. The Scallions menu and logo changes every semester to reflect changing food trends and to allow students to experience a wide range of culture and cuisines. From Greek to Mexican to a taste of Georgia each semester provides a menu that is unique and special. Scallions is open to the general public and walk in are welcome but reservations are definitely recommended.

Grilled Tomato Veggie Soup

4 ea. ripe tomatoes, halved & seeded
½ c. thinly sliced carrot
2 cloves garlic, sliced
6 c. chicken stock
½ tsp. liquid smoke
1 tsp. freshly ground black pepper

½ red bell pepper, large dice and seeded
6 Tbsp. olive oil
½ small yellow onion, sliced
1 c. whipping cream
1 tsp. salt
Dash of chipotle Tabasco sauce

Directions

Preheat the grill pan.

Toss in the onions, carrots and peppers with 3 Tbsp. olive oil and add to the grill pan and grill for 4 to 5 minutes. Add in the garlic and cook for one more minute turning the vegetables over as they grill. Add the grilled vegetables to the stock pot and filled with the chicken stock. Place the seeded tomatoes in a large bowl and toss with 3 Tbsp. of the olive oil. Set the tomatoes cut-side down on the grill and grill for about 3 minutes turning over halfway through the cooking time. Add the tomato to the stock pot and simmer for 20 minutes or until tender. Pass the soup through a food mill and then strain into a saucepan. Add in the cream, liquid smoke, Tabasco and salt and pepper.

Top with a pinch of minced chives.

Submitted by Chef Lou Rice

SKYBOX GRILLE & LOUNGE

1271 East Montclair
Springfield, MO 65804
(417) 877-9595

Skybox is Southwest Missouri's best sports bar and grille. It features more than 20 TVs throughout . With the state of the art kitchen headed up by Chef Robert McLing, Skybox provides different daily lunch specials, along with its main menu that has something for everyone. An outdoor patio, a v.i.p. room and newly added game room provide Skybox customers a great experience every time. Skybox can also handle all your catering needs as well as large or small group parties.

Peacock Salad

This colorful salad resembles a peacock and goes great on a hot summer day!

½ c. tuna or chicken salad
2 oz. fresh pineapple chunks
2 oz. fresh honeydew slices
½ fresh ripe banana
1 maraschino cherry
Servings: 1

3 pieces of leaf lettuce
2 oz. fresh cantaloupe slices
2 oz. fresh watermelon chunks
½ fresh apple
1 toothpick

Directions

Lay 2 pieces of leaf lettuce on a plate, covering the bottom. Place the tuna or chicken salad in the center of the plate using an ice cream scoop. Decoratively arrange the pineapple, cantaloupe, honeydew and watermelon around the salad. Stand the banana upright in the salad for the heck and fasten the cherry to the top with toothpick for the head. Cut the apple into wedges and place on side for wings. Use the remaining pice of leaf lettuce and cut it into a "V" shape as the tail.

Submitted by Robert F. McLing, chef-manager

SMOKEY BONES BARBEQUE & GRILL

2040 E. Independence St.
Springfield, MO 65804
(417) 890-1945

Resembling a rustic mountain lodge, Smokey Bones Barbeque & Grill serves award-winning barbeque and a broad variety of other American favorites. Its menu features slow-smoked Baby-Back and St. Louis-style ribs, hand-pulled pork, sliced beef brisket, choice steaks, grilled chicken and fish, fresh salads, sandwiches, Buffalo burgers and Angus burgers. Some appetizers and side offerings include Barbeque Chicken Nachos, Old-Fashioned Skillet Corn Bread with crushed pecan butter, green beans and cinnamon apples. Guests also enjoy the restaurant's signature dessert – a bag of fresh "made-to-order" hot cinnamon-sugar doughnuts served with strawberry dipping sauce.

Grilled Oregon Pear & Spinach Salad

¼ lb. whole pecans
2 Tbsp. vegetable oil
1 lb. red seedless grapes, washed
½ med. red onion, sliced
1 c. raspberry vinaigrette dressing
  (or vinaigrette dressing)

2 Bosc or Bartlett pears
2 bags leaf spinach (9 oz. ea.), washed
2 c. bleu cheese crumbles
1 c. diced Roma tomatoes
1 15-oz. can mandarin orange segments,
  washed

Directions

Preparation: Chill one large mixing bowl and four large individual salad bowls. Preheat oven to 350° F and preheat charcoal or gas grill to medium-high heat. Set pecans on baking tray and place in oven for 10-15 minutes until dark brown taking care not to burn. Remove pan from oven and set aside to cool. Cut each pear in half lengthwise and remove stem, bottom and seeds. Slice each half into approximately 3/16" slices. Immediately lightly brush oil on each pear slice on both sides, place on grill for approximately 1 minute per side. Remove from grill, place on pan, and chill in refrigerator.

Completing Oregon Pear and Spinach Salad: Cut chilled pear slices in half lengthwise. In large chilled mixing bowl, place spinach, grilled pears, grapes, bleu cheese crumbles, red onion slices, roasted pecans, tomatoes and vinaigrette dressing. Toss well and portion into individual salad bowls. Garnish each salad with ¼ of the drained mandarin oranges.

Submitted by Smokey Bones team

ST. MICHAEL'S

301 South Avenue
Springfield, MO
(417) 865-2315

Although the names have changed over the past 32 years, the style remains consistent. Owner/operators Nick and Jenny Russo have a long standing history in the local restaurant industry. St. Michael's, located at the corner of South and McDaniel, in Springfield, MO, has evolved from Pop's Malt Shop, Ebbets Field (both the Cherry Street and Walnut Street locations) and Russo's Café and Market. Their most recent project is an intimate (65-70 seat) sports eatery located in the heart of the downtown revival. Jenny, a former Kansas City resident, operates St. Michael's during the daytime hours and has developed a reputation for her fresh soups and gourmet sandwiches and currently boasts that she can make 3 sandwiches to her husband's one. Three to two may be a more realistic ratio. St. Michael's continues with their tradition of serving fresh 1/2 pound burgers and fresh-cut fries. The restaurant is available for private gatherings while catering is also available.

Chicken Tortellini Soup

1 celery
Fresh garlic
Extra virgin olive oil
1 small can of whole peeled tomatoes
Salt, pepper, fresh basil and grated Romano cheese

1 carrot
2 bone in chicken breasts
Fresh spinach
6 oz. of cheese filled frozen tortellini

Directions

In a medium pot filled with water cook the two bone in chicken breasts. Once the breasts are cooked allow them to cool. When cool, pull the meat from the bone. Use the water in which the breasts have been cooked as a broth for the soup, about 24 ounces. Add the cooked chicken pieces to the broth. Chop the celery, carrot and cook over a medium heat in the pot with the chicken and the broth. Drain most of the juice from the can of tomatoes. Hand crush the remaining peeled tomatoes, do not blend. Use a high quality tomato (Progresso); an inferior tomato will feel coarse when crushing. Add the tomatoes to the broth. In a separate small pan place enough olive oil to cover the bottom of the pan (low flame); add chopped fresh garlic and basil (amount of garlic will vary to your taste); when garlic is cooked-not brown- add garlic and olive oil to soup. Add salt and pepper to taste. In a medium pot filled with water place tortellini once water has begun to boil. Do not overcook tortellini. Rinse tortellini. Once carrots and celery are cooked, turn off heat on soup and add a handful of fresh spinach and cooked tortellini. When spinach is wilted serve the soup topped with Picarino Romano cheese. Enjoy with a loaf of Italian bread, a side of cheese and a glass of good wine. That's life in 1956 on Atlantic City's Georgia Avenue.

Submitted by Nick & Jenny Russo, owners 44

THE FRISKY FROG

2325 Bittersweet
Lake Ozark, MO 65049
(573) 365-5500

The Frisky Frog Sports Bar is located on the 1st floor of The Horny Toad Entertainment Complex. It features billiards, darts, pinball and arcade games to please the entire family. A fast service restaurant is available for the wandering guest to enjoy. Guests can also enjoy live music, national concerts and plenty of "boat people watching."

Hearty Steak & Vegetable Soup

1½ lb. cubed sirloin
¼ c. vegetable oil
2 med. carrots, diced
1 large white onion, diced
4 ea. celery stalks, diced
½ lb. sliced mushroom

2 bay leaves
1½ qt. demi glaze (found in gourmet shops)
8 oz. red wine
Salt, pepper and granulated garlic to taste
Butter
2 ea. Idaho potato, diced

Directions

Heat demi-glaze, mushroom and bay leaf to low simmer. Season meat with salt, pepper and granulated garlic; pan sear in oil. Discard oil, drain meat and add to demi-glaze. Deglaze pan with red wine and let reduce to syrup. Strain and add to soup. Sauté vegetables in butter and add to soup. When all ingredients are incorporated, add potatoes, adjust seasoning and reduce slowly until potatoes are done. Approximately 20-30 minutes.

Submitted by Stefan Haney, executive chef

WOBBLY BOOTS BBQ

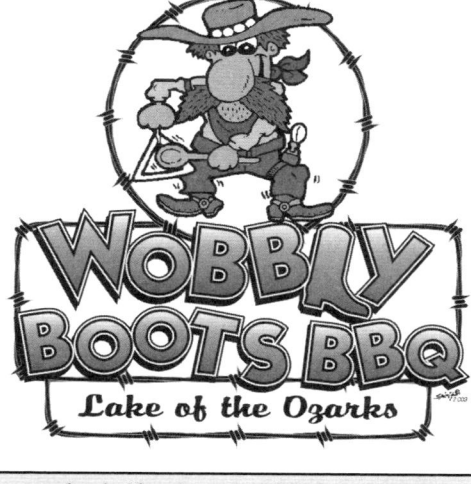

5203 Highway 54
Osage Beach, MO 65065
(573) 348-2277
www.wobblyboots.com

Located a half-mile west of the Grand Glaize Bridge in the heart of Osage Beach. Wobbly Boots BBQ has over 40 awards received including best wings, best barbecue at the lake and Grand Champion of the Iowa Barbeqlossal.

Signature Sauce, Mouthwatering BBQ, Smoked Prime Rib, Black Angus Burgers and Crispy Catfish. Call us for carry out or to cater your next event.

Open Every Root-N-Toot-N Day at 11 a.m.

Brunswick Stew

16 oz. onions
16 oz. celery
2 lb. corn
½ gal. ketchup
1¼ lb. smoked pork
2 cans Rotel
¾ gal. water

4 Tbsp. minced, garlic
2 lb. lima beans
2½ lb. new potatoes, peeled or skins on
1 smoked, deboned chicken
3 Tbsp. chicken base
1 c. franks, red hot sauce
Salt and pepper

Directions

Sautée first three ingredients (onions, garlic, celery). Add remaining ingredients and bring to a boil, stirring often. Simmer until potatoes are tender. Remove and cool. Stew is better on second day after flavors have blended.

Submitted by R.J. Rau

RESTAURANT

Recipes of

ENTRÉES

AGRARIO RESTAURANT

311 S. Patton
Springfield, MO 65806
(417) 865-4255
www.agrariorestaurant.com

Agrario is an upscale contemporary restaurant in the heart of Downtown Springfield, Mo. Housed in a restored livery stable built in 1860, we stayed true to the original architecture while creating a comfortable modern restaurant. We have two major influences when it comes to food. First we use as much local product as possible. This allows us to be sure that our ingredients are as fresh and flavorful as possible. We combine these local ingredients with influences from the entire Mediterranean region (Spain all the way to North Africa) to create contemporary dishes that represent various seasons. For this reason we change our menus seasonally to best represent the products that we are receiving from our farmers.

Seared Pork Tenderloin
With Fig and Hazelnut Sauce and North African Spiced Yams

For Pork:
  1 lb. trimmed & cleaned pork tenderloin
  Salt and pepper to taste
For Sauce:
  8 oz. fresh or dry figs
  4 oz. white wine, dry
  4 oz. whole butter
For Yams:
  3 yams, peeled, large dice
  1 tsp. cinnamon, ground
  1 tsp. cardoman, ground
  ½ c. honey

2 oz. extra virgin olive oil

1 oz. minced garlic
4 oz. roughly chopped hazelnuts

4 oz. whole butter
1 tsp. nutmeg, ground
1 tsp. coriander, ground

Directions

Yams: Steam or lightly boil yams until fork tender. Add all remaining ingredients, whip, cover and let stand to develop full flavor.

Pork and sauce: Cut pork tenderloin into approximately 4 oz. portion. Season with salt and black pepper. Heat oil in large skillet. Brown each side of the pork and finish in the oven at 400˚. When pork is cooked to the desired doneness, pull from oven and remove pork from pan. Add garlic, figs and hazelnuts and lightly saute. Add white wine and reduce by half. Turn off heat and add whole butter and swirl rapidly to incorporate evenly. Serve pork on a bed of yams and top with sauce.

Submitted by John Gray, chef

THE ARGENTINA STEAKHOUSE

1410 E. Republic Rd.
Springfield, MO 65804
(417) 886-8010

The Argentina Steakhouse was established in March 2002 in Springfield, Missouri. The family and original staff from Buenos Aries, Argentina opened this independent restaurant in hopes of introducing the people of Springfield to a true steakhouse in the tradition of great cities. As "Springfield's Premiere Steakhouse" the Argentina Steakhouse strives to offer the highest quality and best service to our patrons.

Beef Tenderloin with Fresh Mushroom Cream Sauce

4 8-oz. center cut filets
1 c. heavy whipping cream
½ tsp. dry oregano
Salt and pepper to taste

2 c. button mushrooms
4 Tbsp. butter
½ tsp. paprika

For chives and bacon mashed potatoes
½ tsp. chopped chives
8 peeled Idaho potatoes
Salt and pepper to taste
Pinch of nutmeg

1 Tbsp. butter
2 tsp. chopped bacon
2 c. milk

Directions

For the filets, grill to temperature (about 3 minutes on each side). For the sauce, melt the butter in a sauce pan, add the mushrooms and cream. Let it cook for two minutes, then add the seasonings turning off the heat.

For mashed potatoes, boil the potatoes, strain really well when soft. Add the butter and start mashing until there's no more chunks of potato and finally add seasonings whipping it well.

Submitted by Michael Cho, owner

AUNT MARTHA'S PANCAKE HOUSE

Aunt Martha's Pancake House

1700 E. Cherokee
Corner of Glenstone & E. Cherokee
Springfield, MO 65804
(417) 881-3505

Martha Haworth whose professional performing name was Aunt Martha opened this restaurant 45 years ago during the time of the Ozark Jubilee. Her musician son "Speedy" Haworth worked with her between engagements. They served among other things a pancake dish created from their own "super secret" recipe. They would sift all of the dry "secret ingredients" together into several gallons of mix and have available for the cook.

Due to Martha's failing health and her son Speedy's music career, the thriving business was sold to a young couple, Swede & Ruth Freeman who bought the restaurant in July 1964. The "super secret" recipe for pancake mix was included in the sale. (Ruth and daughter Brenda still run the restaurant.)

Aunt Martha's Pancake House hasn't changed much since the early days. They're still in the same building, under the same name, still serving delicious, traditional home cooked meals. About the only change has been the expanding menu. They are open Tuesday through Saturday from 5 a.m. to 8 p.m and Sundays until 2 p.m.

Chicken & Dumplings

1 medium chicken
⅓ c. baking powder
3 eggs
Dash of pepper

6 c. flour
2 c. milk
3 tsp. salt

Directions

In a 4 qt. pot or Dutch-oven add the chicken and barely cover with water, add 1 tsp. salt and simmer until the meat is tender. When done, remove the chicken from stock. Let cool then dice into approx. 3 cups.

While chicken is cooking mix flour, baking powder, 2 tsp. salt and dash of pepper with eggs and butter in a bowl. Add milk until the dough stiffens. Roll out and coat with flour, cut into strips. Add into boiling chicken stock. Simmer for about 30 minutes. Add chicken and serve. Serves approximately 15 good sized helpings.

Submitted by Ruth Freeman, owner

AVANZARE ITALIAN DINING

S.E. corner of Glenstone & Sunshine
1908 S. Glenstone
Springfield, MO
(417) 567-3463
www.avanzareitaliandining.com

Exceptional Northern Italian cuisine is the center piece of Avanzare. As you dine with us, you'll find world class chef Tony Garcia prepares each dish with only the finest freshly sourced ingredients, including fresh made bread and desserts. A little bit of Italy sits quietly On The Plaza at Glenstone and Sunshine. Surrounding ourselves with only the best ensures your dining experience at Avanzare is what you anticipate and deserve!

Fruiti di Mare (fish of the sea)

9-11 oz. of mixed fresh seafood – shrimp, calamari, scallops, mussels, crab meat, fish and/or lobster

2 cloves sliced garlic, approx. 1 tsp.   1 Tbsp. olive oil
½ c. dry white wine   1 tsp. fresh basil
1 c. marinara sauce   Pinch red pepper
Salt & pepper to taste   Pre-cooked al dente spaghetti
Chopped fresh Italian parsley

Directions

Heat olive oil in a pan over medium-high heat. Add garlic, lightly brown. Sauté scallops with garlic for 1 minute, then add other seafood, basil, salt, pepper, white wine. Bring to a simmer and continue until all seafood cooked (do not over cook). Add marinara and red pepper. Simmer until sauce thickens. Add pasta and toss. Garnish with fresh parsley.

Submitted by Avanzare Staff

BIERMANN'S GENERAL STORE RESTAURANT

226 N. Main St.
Freistatt, MO 65798
(417) 235-9005
www.biermannsfinedining.com

In 1962, after 78 years of successful enterprising in Freistatt, the doors of Biermann's General Store closed. In 1979 the building was purchased from the grandchildren of H. Biermann and remodeling began for Biermann's General Store Restaurant. The primary goal of the owner, Deena Bottom, was to maintain and restore as much of the General Store as possible. German cuisine was served and Biermann's became a well known and successful restaurant for over 20 years. 2003! New owner and operator Ansel Jay Sitton asks that you dine leisurely and sense the Gemulichkeit, but most importantly enjoy the food we are about to serve you. If you are planning a private banquet, meeting or luncheon, we have facilities to accommodate groups from 20 to 100.

Beef Rolls (Rouladen)

1 lb. bottom round roast beef, cooked
Spice brown mustard
Beef gravy

Pickle spears
Bacon

Directions

Slice roast beef into about ⅛-inch slices. Spread mustard on beef, place pickle spear and a slice of cooked bacon. Roll ingredients inside making a beef roll and hold together with wet toothpick. Place on grill or oven rotating to get all sides warm. Top with beef gravy and serve.

Submitted by Jay Sitton, owner

BIJAN'S SEA & GRILLE

209 E. Walnut St.
Springfield, MO 65806
(417) 831-1480

Bijan's has been open for 9 years. It offers an exhibition kitchen and a martini lounge with a walk in cigar humidor. Bijan's has consistently won awards such as Best Restaurant, Best Service and Best Wine List.

Shrimp Bijan

2 oz. pesto
5 medium prosciutto ham strips

5 large shrimp
1 12" bamboo skewer

Directions

Soak skewers in water for 30 minutes to prevent them from burning. Make pesto, peel and devein shrimp and slice ham. Place 1 oz. pesto in cut side of shrimp and wrap with ham slice and press tail to larger meat end (uncut side) to hold ham in place. Skewer shrimp starting at the base of tail at a 45 degree angle and repeat for rest of the shrimp. Grill over open fire about 7-10 minutes or bake for 10 minutes.

Chicken Bijan

1 8 oz. chicken breast
1½ oz. goat cheese

2 oz. prosciutto ham
2 large basil leaves

Directions

Lay chicken breast between two sheets of plastic wrap and pound flat. On one side place on thin slice of prosciutto, 1½ oz. goat cheese and two large basil leaves–roll together and place toothpick to hold. Sear in hot sauté pan then bake for 15 minutes or until done and garnish with Guinness reduction.

Guinness reduction:
1 c. Guinness beer
1 Tbsp. honey

½ c. balsamic vinegar
½ Tbsp. unsalted butter

Mix all ingredients except the butter in a small sauce pan on low heat. Reduce by ¾ then add butter and continue to heat until butter is incorporated. Cool and serve sauce over chicken (should have consistency of honey).

Alfredo:

In medium heated sauté pan add ½ tsp. olive oil and ½ tsp. garlic and brown. Add ½ cup heavy cream, reduce by half and then add 1½ cups cooked pasta, ¼ cup Parmesan (let Parmesan melt and incorporate) and salt and pepper to taste.

Submitted by Mike Jalili, owner

BREEZES

R E S T A U R A N T

Lodge of Four Seasons
Golf Resort and Spa Shiki
Horseshoe Bend Parkway
Lake Ozark, MO 65049
(573) 365-3000

Breezes Restaurant is a bright and airy place for Breakfast and Lunch, offering both indoor and patio dining. Enjoy a fresh omelette made to order at the bountiful Breakfast Buffet, along with Bacon, Sausage, Biscuits & Gravy, freshly sliced Fruit, Breakfast Pastries, Cereals and more. For Lunch, enjoy a Chicken Berry Feta Salad, a Crabcake Sandwich, or one of our many Health Conscious entrées, inspired by our own nationally renowned Spa Shiki.

Grilled Swordfish with Lime and Cumin

4 Portions (6 oz.) Fresh Swordfish
½ tsp. ground cumin

2 fresh limes

Directions

Rub the Swordfish with fresh lime, then with the ground cumin. Grill the fish over medium-high heat. BE CAREFUL NOT TO OVERCOOK! – Swordfish will quickly become very dry if it is cooked too long.

Serve and enjoy!

Submitted by Gary Leap, HK's Sous Chef

BRUNO'S RESTAURANT

Fine Italian Casual Dining

416 South Ave.
Springfield, MO 65806
(417) 866-0007
www.brunos-restaurant.net

Bruno Gargiulo brings tastes of his Italian home to downtown Springfield. He is making authentic Italian cuisine with the best ingredients he can find. His specialty is Southern Italian cooking. Gargiulo makes almost everything on-site. He and his wife Melissa spend each morning preparing dough for their bread and pizza crusts. "Everything is special on the menu because you won't find it anywhere else," he said. More than 60 Italian wines representing different regions of Italy are offered at Bruno's.

Galletto Arrosto
(Roasted Chicken)

½ small chicken (12 to 15 oz.)
Marinade:
½ c. olive oil
1 Tbsp. thyme
2 lemons, juiced

4 large cloves garlic, minced
1 Tbsp. rosemary

Directions

Combine marinade ingredients thoroughly. Place chicken and marinade in a deep plastic or ceramic covered container, turning chicken to thoroughly coat. Cover and marinate in refrigerator for two to four hours.

To cook: Place marinated chicken in a cast iron pan and over medium-high to high flame, sear the chicken quickly, turning it several times to make sure it is evenly seared, allowing approximately 5 minutes total to each side. Then remove from top heat and transfer the chicken to a 350° oven. Cook uncovered for 20 to 25 minutes. Then serve immediately.

Submitted by Bruno Gargiulo, owner

BURR'S RESTAURANT

2708 South Glenstone Ave.
Springfield, MO 65804
(417) 882-5579

Good Food, Good Spirits, Good Friends

Burr's opened its doors in August of 1985 as a neighborhood restaurant and lounge. We have tried to keep a comfortable and cozy atmosphere which enhances conversation. We specialize in USDA Choice hand cut steaks and fresh seafood.

Burr's Fresh Roast Prime Rib

1 - 12 to 14-lb. choice rib eye roast
4 Tbsp. cracked black pepper
2-3 Tbsp. granulated onion

1 c. Worcestershire sauce
2-3 Tbsp. granulated garlic
1 box (3 lb.) Morton Kosher salt

Directions

Trim fat from rib eye roast and place on a roasting rack in a roasting pan. Coat with Worcestershire sauce then cover with cracked black pepper. Sprinkle with granulated garlic and then with granulated onion.

Take the box of Kosher salt and add enough water to make a paste. Cover the top of the roast with salt paste.

Bake in a 220° oven until the prime rib reaches your desired temperature. 120° very rare, 130°-140° rare, 140°-150° medium rare, 150°-155° medium and 160°-165° medium well.

Let roast cool for 30 minutes, remove salt cap, slice and serve with au jus.

Submitted by Barry Oelschlaeger

CAFE GLAIZE

Inn at Grand Glaize
Hwy. 54, Lake Road 40
Osage Beach, MO 65065
(573) 348-4731

At Café Glaize, our Executive Chef David Harkins and his culinary team take pride in the quality and presentation of each meal. Choose from an array of tempting dishes, we have a wide range of options available – from formal "Gold Medal Dining" to our casual Ozark Barbecue or go casual with finger foods. Banquet services, breakfast meetings, boardroom lunches, carefree themed parties and elaborate ballroom dining can all be catered to suit your needs.

Peppercorn Brandy Beef Tenderloin

2 Tbsp. olive oil
1 lb. beef tenderloin
1 oz. green peppercorns
4 oz. demi glace

2 oz. brandy
1 oz. heavy whipping cream
White pepper
Kosher salt

Directions

Heat skillet on medium, add olive oil. Cut beef into 2 oz. medallions and rub with salt and pepper. Sautee beef medallions on both sides to right under desired temperature. Add green peppercorns and continue sauteeing for 30 seconds. Remove beef medallions from skillet and set aside two medallions on each plate. Add brandy to de glace the skillet. Add demi glace and heavy cream. Reduce sauce on low heat until thickened. Ladle sauce over beef medallions. Serves 4.

Submitted by David E. Harkins, executive chef

CHATEAU GRILLE

At Chateau on the Lake Resort
415 North State Hwy 265
Branson, MO 65616
(417) 334-1161
www.chateauonthelake.com

CHATEAU GRILLE
AT CHATEAU ON THE LAKE

Featuring a stunning view of Table Rock Lake, the Chateau Grille boasts a truly matchless fine-dining experience. Known for its elegant presentation and exceptional cuisine, the Chateau Grille offers deliciously prepared, exquisitely presented American grill selections. Join us in the Chateau Grille for breakfast, lunch, teatime, or for a memorable evening dining experience.

Chateau Chicken Vanilla

Jumbo Shrimp Encased in Scallop and Spinach Mousseline, Stuffed inside a Breast of Chicken and Pastry, Finished with a Sauce of Madagascar Vanilla Bean

For Mousseline:
8 oz. Scallops
1 Tsp. Old Bay Seasoning
2 Ea. Egg Whites
1 Tbsp. heavy cream

Put all ingredients together in a food processor and puree until mix well.

For Chicken Breast:
6 ea. chicken breast, boneless, Skinless, 6 oz., Pounded
6 ea. shrimp 21/25, raw
½ inch Julienne strip
2 sheet puff pastry, cut into 4 triangles
1 c. Mousseline (see recipe)
Baby spinach leaves
1 ea. roasted pimento
1½ tsp. Chateau seasoning
4 ea. egg yolks

Put about 2 tablespoon of mousseline onto each chicken breast and spread evenly. Lay out 8 leaves of baby spinach evenly over mousseline. Put 1 strip of roasted pimento in middle. Break shrimp so it won't curl up when cooked, and put that over the pimento. Start wraps chicken like making a roulade. Season each chicken breast with chateau seasoning and start wrapping them with the puff pastry triangles. This should resemble a croissant. Brush with whipped eggs yolks.

For the Sauce:
1 c. Madeira wine
1 ea. shallot, fine diced
1 qt. heavy cream
10 ea. Madagascar vanilla beans
½ c. blonde roux
3 ea. bay leaf
4 sprigs thyme, fresh
2 qts. chicken stock
4 tsp. Kosher salt
½ tsp. white pepper

Directions

Pre-heat oven to 350°. Lay wrap chicken onto the baking pan line with parchment paper. Brush each chicken thoroughly with egg wash. Put chicken in oven and bake for 25 minutes or until done. (When done, the puff pastry should be nice and golden brown on top.) Let chicken rest for about 5 minutes before serving.

Submitted by Chef Anthony J. Burke, C.E.C.

1212 Linn St
Sikeston, MO 63801
(573) 471-2006

Cheer's bar and grill began business in 1990 in a small 1500 sq. ft. building with approximately 4 employees. It has since grown into a 5000 sq. ft. building with 22 employees. We specialize in several areas. We have choice steaks, which are some of the best around. We also serve items not easily found in our area, such as cajun dishes, Mexican dishes, homemade burgers, tamales and a variety of fish and seafood. All our food is homemade! We also have a full bar. Come by and see our lake and the ducks our back of our sunroom. It's beautiful and makes for romantic dining.

Chicken Pomodora

3 Tbsp. olive oil
¼ c. vodka
Juice from 3 lemons
Cream soup base (powder form) or
   or cornstarch to thicken
½ c. cauliflower florets

3 Tbsp. flour
½ gal. chicken broth or chicken base
   with water
½ c. tomatoes, chopped
½ c. broccoli florets

Directions

Heat 3 Tbsp. of olive oil in pan. Add 3 Tbsp. flour and lightly brown. Add ¼ c. vodka and mix thoroughly. Then add ½ gal. of water with chicken base of ½ gal. of chicken broth. Squeeze in juice from 3 lemons.

Thicken to make sauce with a cream soup powder base or with cornstarch. Then at the end add ½ c. chopped tomatoes, ½ c. broccoli florets and ½ c. cauliflower florets.

Lightly bread and flour boneless chicken breast and pan sear until chicken is done. Put chicken breast on plate and pour sauce over it.

Submitted by Joyce Winchester, owner

CHURCHILL COFFEE COMPANY

1604 E. Republic Road
Springfield, MO 65804
(417) 823-8203

Churchill Coffee Company is a locally owned and operated company producing the finest coffee, tea, chai, and hot chocolates. In addition to our award-winning coffees, Churchill has a large selection of food items: sandwiches, wraps, soups and salads. Our award-winning desserts are the perfect compliment to your food and drink experience. We can also cater any event. Call ahead and reserve our meeting room. It's the ideal place for any business meeting, baby shower, birthday party, or any special event. Let us provide you with ultimate coffee and food experience.
Churchill Coffee—IT JUST TASTES BETTER!!!

Honey Pecan Chicken

2½ oz. green onions
4 oz. diced celery
2½ oz. crushed pecans
1½ lbs. cooked diced chicken

7 oz. *Honey mustard dressing*
  2½ oz. French's honey mustard
  4½ oz. honey

Directions

Mix all ingredients together until evenly mixed. Serve on sandwiches, salads, in wraps or as a dip with chips or crackers.

Submitted by Sheila Randolph, general manager

CLARION HOTEL SPRINGFIELD

BY CHOICE HOTELS

Banquets & Catering

3333 S. Glenstone
Springfield, MO 65804
(417) 883-6550
www.clarionhotel-spfld.com

The Clarion Hotel & Conference Center features 193 guestrooms including Suites & a Jacuzzi Suite. It offers over 17,000 sq. feet of meeting space. The conference center can accommodate groups from 10 to 700 guests. It's the perfect location for Corporate Meetings, Weddings, Reunions and Social Events. Being locally owned and operated, the Clarion has established a reputation of providing excellent guest service, excellent accommodations and delicious food.

Potato Encrusted Chicken

4 boneless skinless chicken breasts
½ stick melted butter
1 tsp. garlic salt

8 oz. frozen hash brown
2 oz. grated Parmesan
1 tsp. parsley

Directions

Preheat oven to 400°. Allow hash browns to thaw. Toss hash browns with garlic salt, parsley, and Parmesan. Toss again with melted butter. Place chicken on lightly oiled sheet pan. Top loosely with seasoned hash browns (do not pack) and place in oven. Bake for 30 min. Remove when golden brown and chicken is cooked.

Submitted by Chef John Blansit

1201 E. 32nd St.
Joplin, MO 64804
(417) 626-0032

At Club 1201 the atmosphere is very much contemporary, in shades of grey with an ongoing theme of doors and glass. The food is wonderful with a strong emphasis on fresh ingredients. Daily Lunch & Gourmet Pizza Specials, Open 7 Days a Week. In-House Banquet Facilities/Out-Of-House Catering.

The San Lorenzo

Burger:
1 lb. ground beef
1 tsp. dried chipotle chilis
1 tsp. ground black pepper
Avocado Salsa:
2 c. chopped roma tomato
½ c. fresh chopped cilantro
1 tsp. Kosher salt
Dash of your favorite tequila

2 Tbsp. dark chili powder
2 tsp. Kosher salt
1 tsp. granulated garlic

½ c. chopped red onion
2 Tbsp. fresh lime
1 c. peeled, chopped avocado
2 garlic cloves, minced

4 2-oz. multigrain hamburger buns
Avocado Salsa

Directions

Prepare grill. First, take the dried chipotle chiles, and re-hydrate them. Then, combine the beef, dark chile powder, chipotle chiles, kosher salt, ground black pepper, and granulated garlic in a bowl. Work all the ingredients well together by kneading the beef with your hands. Once they are combined, begin making the patties.

Submitted by Meg Shelfer, kitchen manager

DEVIL'S POOL RESTAURANT

Big Cedar Lodge Resort
612 Devil's Pool Rd.
Ridgedale, MO 65739
(417) 335-2777
www.big-cedar.com

There is no mystery as to what attracted entrepreneur Jude Simmons to this slice of Ozarks wilderness. The gentle hillsides were an ideal backdrop for his rustic getaway that would reflect the grandeur of Adirondacks lodges and entertain in casual elegance. The home featured native materials, including a huge stone fireplace that still warms our dining room when fall and winter chill the air. Today, hand wrought metal chandeliers cast a warm glow over antique furnishings and our 100 year old mahogany bar. Bark covered logs and exposed rafters are a fitting complement to the sporting gear and animal mounts that adorn our walls in the Bass Pro tradition.

Kentucky Braised Short Ribs

10 lb. short ribs 2½-in. cut
Salt and pepper to taste
2½ gal. beef stock
¼ c. garlic, chopped
For the glaze:
   8 oz. Markers Mark Bourbon
   2 c. stoneground mustard

Flour, as needed
1 gal. tomato paste
Salad oil, as needed
Roux, as need

2 qts. sorghum syrup

Directions

Dredge ribs in seasoned flour. Pan sear in hot oil in tilt skillet, until dark brown. Remove ribs and place in a deep pan. Make sure the bones are sticking up. Add mire poix to tilt skillet and sauté until caramelized then add tomato paste, and garlic. Continue cooking until all ingredients are well caramelized. Add stock. Pour stock and vegetables over bones to cover. Cover and place in oven at 250° for 4-6 hours. Check every hour to make sure bones are covered with liquid. If needed, add water. When ribs are tender (easily removed from the bone), pull out of stock and place on a sheet pan to cool. Strain stock, return to stove and thicken with roux. Adjust seasoning with salt and pepper, strain sauce. Pull bones off of ribs.

For the glaze: Mix all ingredients in a bowl, and wait until ready to serve and ladle onto the ribs.

Submitted by Todd Leonard, asst. food and beverage director

DOG DAYS BAR & GRILL

1232 Jeffries Road, 19 MM by water
Osage Beach, MO 65065
573-348-9797
www.dogdays.ws

Proclaiming itself as being for "young people of all ages," this restaurant and bar features Tropically Infused Dishes as well as steaks, seafood and sandwiches. Dog Days offers live Blues and Rock & Roll music Wednesday through Sunday nights.

Gulf Coast Grouper

1 6-8 oz. grouper fillet
½ Tbsp. Cajun seasoning
3 oz. crawfish tail meat
3-4 oz. heavy cream

½ Tbsp. Key West seasoning
½ Tbsp. garlic
1 oz. Grand Marnier
rice

Directions

Season Grouper Filet with Key West Season and place on preheated grill. While fish is cooking saute garlic, crawfish, and Cajun seasoning. Deglaze pan with Grand Marnier add Heavy cream and reduce, add salt and pepper to taste. When Grouper is finished place on bed of rice and pour sauce over the top finish with green onions.

Submitted by R.J. Rau

167 Hwy. 165
Branson, MO 65616
(417) 335-5060

BRANSON'S "HOME OF THE TOSSED ROLLS"

Home of Rudy the Roll Tosser and those melt-in-your-mouth, fresh-baked dinner rolls! Delicious home-style cooking and fast, friendly service. Choose from hand-breaded and deep-fried catfish, juicy wood-fired steaks, ribs, burgers and more. Kids menu. Open daily 11 a.m. - 9 p.m.

Scallop & Shrimp Pasta

3 ea. (21/25) shrimp
2 oz. tomatoes
1 oz. tarragon
2 oz. Parmesan
7 oz. long pasta
Pinch salt and pepper

4 ea. scallops
2 oz. asparagus
6 oz. white wine cream sauce
2 oz. clarified butter
2 oz. white wine

Directions

Heat the pan with butter, add the scallops, sear the scallops, add the shrimps, saute. Add the asparagus, tomatoes and tarragon. Deglaze with white wine, add white wine cream sauce. Drop the pasta in the water, drain well. Saute together, place in the bowl, garnish with Parmesan and basil.

Submitted by Fall Creek staff

FAMOUS DAVE'S

**New Location
At Branson Landing
Branson, MO
COMING SOON**

The recipe is part of a collection of "Down Home" cooking in Dave's fabulous book Famous Dave's Backroads and Sidestreets (proceeds from the book benefit charity).

Famous Dave's Twice-Smoked Orgasmic Ham

1 smoked, bone-in ham, 12-15 lbs.
Pineapple slices

Whole cloves
Maraschino cherries

Glaze
1 c. frozen tangerine juice concentrate
½ c. French Pommery mustard
½ c. Dijon mustard
1 tsp. ground cloves
½ tsp. cayenne

1 c. all fruit apricot preserves (Dave likes to use Polaner)
1 c. packed light brown sugar
½ tsp. coarsely ground black pepper

Directions

Use the indirect method of slow-cooking, so get your grill ready for this recipe and follow the link for cooking directions.

Score the ham in a cross diamond pattern. Stud the ham with whole cloves at each cross intersection.

Smoke at 225° F for 3 hours. Remove ham and place on a sheet pan. Secure the pineapple slices and cherries to the ham with toothpicks.

To make the glaze, combine glaze ingredients and mix well. Generously slather ham with glaze and bake in a 350° F oven for 1½ hours. Brush with the ham glaze every 20 minutes or so. Remove from oven and let rest for 30 minutes before serving.

Submitted by Famous Dave

Ristorante

GILARDI'S

820 East Walnut
Springfield, MO 65806
(417) 862-6400

Nicola Gilardi began his career in the culinary arts at the family's restaurant in Italy. Upon learning the importance of a strong work ethic, he decided to pursue his dream of owning his own restaurant. "Every customer of mine is not only treasured for the existence of my business but also as a friend. My employees and I strive to provide the best Italian dining experience possible," says Nicola.

"My business thrives on people who are regulars. About ninety percent of our customer base are regulars. The remaining ten percent will be after the first dinner".

Linguine Al Pesto

Pesto:
6 c. basil loosely packed
4 oz. Parmesan cheese
1 clove garlic, chopped

2½ oz. pine nuts
2½ c. olive oil

Directions

Combine: basil, pine nuts, Parmesan cheese, oil, garlic, pepper and salt to taste and put in the blender or food processor until everything is blended together.

Linguine Pasta:
1 lb. linguine
1 c. potatoes cut in small squares

1 c. green beans cut in half
4 qts. salted water

Directions

Bring 4 qts. of water and 2 Tbsp. of salt to a boil. Add linguine. Make sure you move the pasta around so it doesn't stick together. Cook for 6 minutes and then add potatoes and green beans. Strain the pasta and keep hot. Put in big bowl and combine pasta and pesto.

Submitted by Nicola Gilardi, chef/owner

HEMINGWAY'S BLUE WATER CAFE

Located on the 4th floor of Bass Pro Shops
1935 S. Campbell
Springfield, MO 65898
(417) 891-5100
www.hemingwaysbluewatercafe.com

Hemingway's Blue Water Cafe is a Fantastic place to eat for any occasion. We have a variety of Entrees' for an unforgettable meal. We provide a fine dining experience in a unique casual atmosphere showcasing a 30,000 gallon saltwater tank and numerous exotic displays. Our culinary features include a vast array of seafood and freshwater fish as well as steaks, pork chops, and chicken dishes. A kids menu is also available. In addition to our high quality menu items, we offer a buffet for breakfast, lunch, and dinner Monday through Saturday as well as a brunch buffet on Sundays.

Venison Grand Veneur

24 oz. trimmed venison loin
½ lb. sliced bacon
1 Tbsp. olive oil
Marinade:
  ½ gal. red wine
  Carrots, sliced
  ½ head celery, diced
  1 med. onion, sliced
  1 bunch fresh parsley, chopped

1 Tbsp. butter
½ Tbsp. salt
1 Tbsp. cracked black pepper

1 garlic clove, chopped
3 pinches salt
1 Tbsp. cracked black pepper
2 Tbsp. red wine vinegar

Directions

Salt and pepper the venison loin and soak in the marinade overnight. When ready to cook, wrap the loin with slices of bacon and tie with twine. Strain the marinade and keep vegetables on the side. Heat a large skillet, add olive oil and butter and when the butter turns to a golden grown, sear the loin on all four sides and remove. Sauté the marinated vegetables in the same skillet utilizing the drippins from the loin until light brown. Place the vegetables in a roasting pan.

Add remaining marinade to a sauté pan, bring to a boil and reduce to half. Pour the reduced marinade into the roasting pan with the vegetables. Place venison loin on top of the vegetables. Braise at 375° for 10 minutes. Periodically, baste venison with juices and continue cooking for 5 to 10 minutes or until desired temperature is reached.

Slice the loin and serve with Grand Veneur sauce accompanied with a bouqettiere of fresh vegetables and Shitake and Oyster mushroom sautéed in garlic and olive oil.

Submitted by Chef Marcel Bonetti, CEC, AAC

1364 E. Battlefield
Springfield, MO 65805
(417) 883-3033

Heritage Cafeteria is still home-owned and operated since its beginning in 1960. Known for home-style comfort foods, the fried chicken can't be beat. Roast beef, real mashed potatoes, homemade rolls and desserts are all made fresh daily. "Fine food and gracious dining is our proud heritage."

Beef Pepper Steak

2 lbs. thin sliced sirloin tips
2 qts. onions sliced in strips
1 lb. white rice (raw weight)

2 qts. sliced green peppers
2 qts. fresh mushrooms sliced

Marinade:
1 c. teriyaki sauce
¼ c. vegetable oil

⅓ c. soy sauce

Brown sauce:
Marinade left from above
1 c. beef stock

2 tsp. corn starch
2 tsp. water

Directions

Marinate made in soy sauce, teriyaki sauce and oil for approximately 45 minutes, drain and reserve marinade for brown sauce.

Dissolve corn starch in cold water to make paste. Bring beef stock and the marinade to a boil.

Add cornstarch mixture to step 2 and bring to a boil, then reduce to a simmer and cook until clear and thickened.

Grill mixture of meat and vegetables on a hot grill. Vegetables should be crisp.

Pour brown sauce over grill mixture, serve with white rice.

Submitted by Don Evans, owner

HICKOK'S STEAKHOUSE & BREWERY

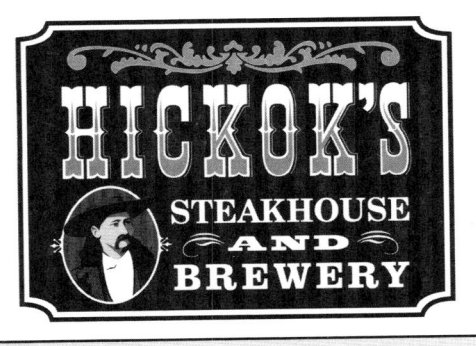

314 S. Patton
Springfield, MO 65804
(417) 872-1141
www.hickokssteakhouse.com

Family friendly, fun, and Affordable. The newest steakhouse in town. Hickok's Steakhouse and Brewery. Come visit the old west in one of the oldest buildings in downtown Springfield only a block from where the famous gunfight between Wild Bill Hickok and Dave Tutt happened in 1865. The first fast draw gunfight in America. Great Food, Great Beer, Great Fun, Lunch or Dinner Monday through Saturday. All at a Great Price. Hickok's Steakhouse and Brewery.

Southwestern Chicken Cordon Bleu
This southwestern take on traditional cordon bleu is best served with roasted jalapeno potato skins topped with a black bean and corn salsa.

6 boneless, skinless chicken breasts
Stuffing:
  1 lb. hot chorizo
  1 red bell pepper, diced
  2 c. asadero (or Velveeta) cheese, grated
  1 c. flour (all-purpose)
Egg wash:
  6 eggs
Queso sauce:
  2 lbs. Velveeta
  ¼ c. cilantro

1 med. yellow onion, diced
6 clove garlic, minced
½ c. cilantro, chopped
6 c. Japanese bread crumbs

1 c. milk

1 c. salsa
1 c. milk

Directions

Brown chorizo, drain excess fat and set aside. In the same pan melt butter, soften onion and red bell pepper. Add garlic and cook until aromatic (about 1 minute). Add cilantro, salt and pepper to taste, add chorizo and grated cheese then let cool.

Make a linear incision with a pairing knife in the thickest part of the breast creating a "pocket." Stuff "pocket" with chorizo mixture and freeze. Combine eggs, milk and whip thoroughly. Take frozen breast, dredge in flour, then egg wash, then bread crumbs and then back into egg wash, then back into bread crumbs (double breading ensures a good seal). Deep fry until golden brown and finish in a 350° oven until internal temperature reaches 140°. Serve drizzled with queso sauce.

Submitted by Kevin Sparks, chef de cuisine

72

302 E. Walnut
Springfield, MO 65806
(417) 865-0366
www.izumihatake.net

Izumi Hatake is the only Japanese sushi and grill restaurant in downtown Springfield. It has been in business for over 5 years and is well-known for contemporary Japanese cuisine. Come and experience the uniqueness of our specially prepared sushi and various dishes.

Negimaki
(Green onion roll)

4 oz. sirloin steak
2 tsp. corn starch
½ tsp. salt
1 c. vegetable oil

2 pieces green onion
1 egg
½ tsp. pepper

Directions

Add ½ tsp. of salt and ½ tsp. of pepper into a small bowl with 1 egg. Scramble and mix together. Beat the 4 oz. sirloin steak until it flattens to about 2-3 mm thick.

Cut the roots off the 2 green onions and wrap them with the sirloin steak. Now cover the whole steak with 2 tsp. of corn starch and soak them in the scrambled eggs.

Deep fry in the vegetable oil for about 2 or 3 minutes at 350°.

Submitted by Jungil Paik

LUIGI'S PIZZA KITCHEN

1447 Highway 248, Branson, MO 65616 - (417) 339-4544
1972 Highway 165, Branson, MO 65616 - (417) 334-3344
107 W. Aldersgate Rd., Nixa, MO 65714 - (417) 725-3336
www.luigispizzakitchen.com

Luigi's Pizza Kitchen, a locally owned and operated Italian Restaurant that also delivers. Specializing in St. Louis style thin crust pizza, we also offer New York style hand tossed as well. With over 30 toppings, traditional and gourmet, there is certainly a pizza for everyone. We have twelve different gourmet pizzas and the list keeps growing as our culinary team continues to create new innovations in pizza. We also have a large selection of pastas, sandwiches, salads, appetizers and entrees. With two locations in Branson we are close to you for either dine in, carryout or delivery. Voted Best Dining in Branson by 417 Magazine, we guarantee you'll love our food as well.

Luigi's Fettuccine Alfredo

1 pt. heavy cream
Salt and pepper
1 lb. fettuccine pasta (precooked weight)

2 Tbsp. Real butter
½ c. freshly grated Parmigiano Reggiano cheese (find in deli area of your store)

Directions

In a sauce pot, on medium-hi setting, heat butter, cream, salt and pepper, and cooked pasta. Bring to a boil, watch cream as it rises, when cream begins to fall (reduce), pull from heat and mix in Parmigiano cheese. Keep stirring until proper thickness of sauce, (Thick but still a sauce, not paste) If sauce is too thick, DO NOT add more cream. Thin with chicken broth or warm water, not too much. Follow directions on package to cook fettuccine pasta.

This is a simple sauce that you can add many other spices or variations for your own flavors. Example: Hot sauce, lemon juice, any Italian herbs, garlic.

Mangia Bene (Eat Well)

Submitted by Christopher Jordan

METROPOLITAN GRILL

2931 East Battlefield
Springfield, MO 65807
(417) 889-4951

This recipe represents my love for great seafood and Tequila! I was born and raised in northern New Mexico and I am Spanish. I learned to cook in the central coastal area of California. My style is the Mediterranean meets Mexico, and it is a lot of fun.

"Love"

(Blackened Scallops, Grilled Tuna and Shrimp in a Tequila Lime Sauce)

2 3-oz. cuts of Shashimi grade tuna
4 large shrimp, pealed and deveined
2 oz. roses lime juice
½ c. heavy whipping cream
1 Tbsp. butter
Pinch salt and pepper
¼ c. cajun seasoning

6 sea scallops
2 oz. tequila
½ c. chicken stock
Cream
1 tsp. chopped garlic
3 oz. olive oil

Directions

In a small sauté pan heat olive oil. Then after scallops have been dredged in cajun seasoning, cook on medium heat until scallops are cooked through (160°) Grill tuna to desired temperature. Grill shrimp until done.

In a medium sauté pan on medium heat place lime juice, cream, butter seasonings, tequila, garlic and olive oil and bring to a boil until sauce thickens.

CHICKEN STOCK:
½ c. chicken broth
½ Tbsp. olive oil
1 Tbsp. cornstarch

⅛ c. white wine
¼ c. cold water

Bring broth, wine and oil to a boil. Mix starch and water until starch has no lumps. Add starch to boiling broth slowly until it thickens. Then remove from heat.

Submitted by Pat and Jennifer Duran, owners

Inside the IMAX Complex
3562 Shepherd of the Hills Expressway
Branson, MO 65616
(417) 336-4680

The Ozarks are famous for two things – music and food. The spectacular IMAX Film Ozarks Legacy & Legend documents the musical history of the Ozarks by following the McFarlain family over six generations. Here at McFarlain's, we bring to you the culinary history of the Ozarks with traditional Ozark cooking and recipes that have been handed down from generation to generation. A special place where you can sit back, enjoy your meal and our warm hospitality...for breakfast, lunch and dinner!

Ma Hewlett's Meatloaf

2 lbs. ground beef
2 eggs
¾ c. cracker crumbs
½ c. chopped green peppers
1 tsp. Worcestershire sauce
½ tsp. black pepper

1 c. milk
¾ c. bread crumbs
¾ c. chopped onions
½ c. grated carrots
1 Tbsp. salt
½ c. Catsup

Directions

Mix well. Form loaf, place in greased baking dish, cover with plastic wrap and foil.

Bake at 350° for 1 hour. Remove from oven. Drain grease. Cover with catsup sauce and bake for 10 more minutes.

Catsup sauce:
1 cup catsup
1 Tbsp. dry mustard

½ cup brown sugar

Submitted by Debby Black, general manager

McGUFFEY'S RESTAURANT & BAR

2600 W. Hwy. 76
Branson, MO 65616
(417) 336-3600
www.mcguffeys.com

McGuffey's is proud to offer a recipe created exclusively for us by a famous Cajun chef. The New Orleans Seafood Delight is our #1 rated dish as taste tested by our guests. We make our own blackening spice from a secret recipe, but there are several good packaged varieties that will work.

New Orleans Seafood Delight

4 yellow fin tuna steaks, deboned center cut
1 green onion, chopped
1 c. whipping cream
1 c. Parmesan cheese, dry powder
1 Tbsp. blackening spice, to taste

30 shrimp, small, peeled & deveined
1 red pepper, chopped
1 c. half & half
½ lb. butter
1 Tbsp. garlic, fresh chopped
Rice pilaf or cooked pasta

Directions

For the Alfredo: Place ½ tsp. of blackening spice, garlic, half & half, heavy cream, Parmesan cheese and butter in a double boiler on low heat. Whip occasionally & cook until thickened.

Heat a heavy cast iron skillet for 20 minutes. Dip each tuna steak in butter and sprinkle with blackening spice. Fry until steak is medium to medium rare with a light crust on the outside.

In a sauté pan with a little butter, sauté shrimp until white. Add alfredo sauce, red pepper & green onion. Turn off heat. Place tuna steaks atop rice pilaf or pasta & top with a generous portion of shrimp sauce.

Submitted by Paul Militello, GM

MIKAYLA'S GRILLE

At Millwood Golf and Racquet Club
3700 E. Millwood Drive
Ozark, MO 65721
(417) 889-1898

Award winning Mikayla's Grille is located at the beautiful Millwood Golf and Racquet Club. Featuring a wood-burning grill, Mikayla's is known for its Prime Rib and grilled steaks. Sam Hudgins, the Executive Chef designs the menu around contemporary and regional cuisine, with a selection of fresh seafood's, entrees and salads. Mikayla's Grille features a well-rounded wine selection, out door dining and full bar service. The views around the restaurant are breathtaking with lakes, waterfalls and the championship golf course.

Pan Glazed Apple-wood Chicken

Seasoned Flour:

2 c. flour
1 Tbsp. parsley, chopped
1 tsp. Kosher salt
3 oz. sugar
1 tsp. granulated garlic
1 tsp. black pepper

Combine and whisk to aerate.

Hot Apple-wood Bacon Dressing:

4 oz. apple-wood bacon, cooked, chopped
1 c. sugar
2 Tbsp. corn starch
4 oz. white onion, julienne
1 c. cider vinegar
1 c. chicken stock

Sauté the bacon to render fat. Add onion and cook until translucent. Add sugar and caramelize. Deglaze with cider vinegar, slowly simmer. Add the cornstarch to the chicken stock, whisk and add to the bacon liquid. Bring to a boil and set aside once thickened.

The Chicken:

2 oz. olive oil
6 oz. chicken breast, split at lobe
3 oz. chicken stock
1 c. seasoned flour
3 oz. hot apple-wood bacon dressing
1 oz. leek

Heat a sauté pan and add oil. Dredge the chicken in the seasoned flour, shake off excess flour. Sauté at medium high, to sear and caramelize the chicken, flip. Add the chicken stock and hot bacon dressing, reduce the liquid by ½. This will form the glaze while braising the seared chicken. Serve with grilled or sautéed vegetables and rice or infused mashed potatoes.

Submitted by Chef Samuel T. Hudgins, CEC

MOLLIE'S CAFE & BAR

11 South Spanish
Cape Girardeau, MO 63703
(573) 339-1661

Mollie's Cafe & Bar was established in 1989. It is currently owned and operated by Michael Risch and Matt Tygett who operated it for several years before buying it in 2002.

Pork Osso Bucco
In a tomato ragout sauce w/fettuccini alfredo and sautéed vegetables

6 pork shanks
2 Tbsp. salt
3 carrots, diced
1 bunch of celery, diced
¼ c. butter
⅛ c. fresh basil
⅛ c. thyme

2 Tbsp. garlic
2 Tbsp. pepper
2 onions, diced
20 oven roasted tomatoes
4 c. water
⅛ c. parsley
⅛ c. oregano

Directions

Take pork shanks and lightly flour, salt and pepper them. Using a large skillet on medium high, heat braise each side until medium browned. Braise both sides. Take out and set aside. Roast tomatoes in oven for 20 minutes on 300°.

Ragout: take diced carrots, onions and celery. Sauté on medium heat in butter, garlic, salt and pepper for about 5 minutes. Add oven roasted tomatoes, 4 c. of water, parsley, oregano and braised pork shanks. Let simmer for 20-25 minutes on medium high heat stirring every 2 minutes. It should be slightly thickened and meat should be tender. Serves 6.

Alfredo Sauce:

1 qt. heavy cream
1 Tbsp. pepper
2 c. Parmesan cheese

1 Tbsp. salt
½ tsp. nutmeg
8 c. cooked fettuccini

In a large sauce pan, add heavy cream, salt, pepper and nutmeg. Let reduce until slightly thickened. On medium heat whisk in Parmesan cheese until thickened. Add fettuccini. Toss and serve with sautéed vegetables and set Pork Osso Bucco on the fettuccini and vegetables with ragout sauce on top. Sprinkle with Parmesan.

Submitted by Michael Risch, owner

313 S. Patton
Springfield, MO 65806
(417) 865-1188
www.pattonalleypub.com

Patton Alley Pub is Springfield's downtown place to hang out with friends, listen to live music and have a great meal! With over 34 beers on tap, it's the place to be downtown! Patton Alley Pub was voted Best Bar, Best Bar Food, Best Happy Hour and Best Beer Menu by 417 Magazine readers.

Beef and Guinness

5 lbs. cubed beef
Salt and pepper to taste
1 Tbsp. oil

2 qts. Guinness Stout
6 bay leaves

Roux:
½ c. butter, melted   ½ c. flour
(cook in saute pan, stirring constantly until color of peanut butter)

Directions

Coat bottom of stock pot with 1 Tbsp. oil. Brown meat in batches making sure not to crowd the bottom of pan. Place all beef back in pot, add salt and pepper and Guinness Stout. Bring to a boil, constantly skimming any scum off top of liquid. Reduce heat and add bay leaves. Simmer until meat is fork tender. Thick with a roux.

Submitted by Dean Scefonaf, chef

PECKERS GOURMET GRILL & BAR

Gourmet Grill & Bar

3285 Bagnell Dam Blvd.
Lake Ozark, MO 65049
(573) 365-4085

Peckers Gourmet Grill & Bar has a fun family atmosphere, game room, and big screen for all your favorite sports. Breakfast served Saturday and Sunday. The Best Happy Hour at the Lake of the Ozarks.

Tortilla Crusted Tilapia with Chili-Lime Sauce

4 - 7 oz. Tilapia filets
¼ c. flour
1½ c. heavy cream
2 Tbsp. sweet Thai chili sauce
Salt and white pepper to taste

¼ c. crushed white tortilla chips
2 Tbsp. olive oil
4 Tbsp. lime juice
1 Tbsp. cold butter

Directions

In a medium sauce pan bring 2 Tbsp. sweet chili sauce, 4 Tbsp. lime juice, 1½ c. heavy cream to a slow boil reducing by half. In a shallow pan combine tortilla chips and flour, dredge tilapia through crusted. In a large saute pan on medium heat add 2 Tbsp. olive oil and brown fish cooking thoroughly on both sides about 3 minutes. After reducing sauce by half, whisk in cold butter and adjust seasoning. Serve sauce over fish.

Submitted by Laurie Haney, executive chef

PICKLED PETE'S SPORTS BAR & GRILL

5276 Hwy. 54
Osage Beach, MO 65065
(573) 302-8800

Pickled Pete's Sports Bar & Grill is a full service family restaurant established in Jan. 2000. With 32 TVs scattered around (including the bathrooms) there's no chance to miss a play. Many sports packages are carried on satellite so locals and out-of-towners alike get to watch their favorite teams. With a warm atmosphere and friendly staff, Pickled Pete's creates a home-away-from-home for guests to enjoy their dining experience. Everyone that has been to Pickled Pete's would have to tell you that the reason they keep coming back is the food. Most menu items are made from scratch and taste like grandma's cooking. There is a wide variety of choices – sandwiches, steaks, seafood and pasta. There's something to please any tastebud.

Chicken & Portabella Pasta

5 oz. diced chicken
2 Tbsp. butter
½ tsp. kosher salt
1 oz. white wine
8 oz. cooked pasta (your choice)

4 oz. sliced portabella mushrooms
1 tsp. chopped garlic
½ tsp. white pepper
1 Tbsp. Parmesan cheese
¾ c. heavy whipping cream

Directions

Sauté butter, chicken, mushrooms, salt and pepper for 3 minutes on medium. Add garlic and continue for 1 minute. Add white wine and deglaze pan. Add heavy cream and reduce by half. Add Parmesan cheese and pour over noodles.

Submitted by Bryan Peterson

RASTA GRILL

319 W. Walnut
"Downtown" Springfield, MO
(417) 831-7221

Rasta Grill has been a staple of "Downtown" Springfield for close to 10 years. What started out as a 20 seat diner has grown into a 200 seat, full service restaurant. Our full menu of chicken, seafood, steaks, pastas and many other "fusion" dishes, coupled with a large selection of beer, wine and liquor, are offered for a quick lunch or a nice dinner with the family. We look forward to serving Springfield for another 10 years.

Blackened Steak Fettuccini

1 8-oz. strip
10 oz. cooked fettuccini
¼ oz. bell pepper

1 Tbsp. jerk seasoning
6 oz. white sauce

Directions

Cover steak in jerk seasoning and grill to the desired temperature. Grill bell peppers and heat white sauce in a sauté pan. Toss fettuccini noodles in white sauce and garnish with peppers.

Blackened Shrimp Pesto

8 21-25 shrimp peeled and deveined
2 Tbsp. pesto
1 Tbsp. jerk seasoning
1 oz. diced tomatoes

6 oz. white sauce
½ Tbsp. Creole seasoning
10 oz. cooked fettuccini noodles
½ oz. basil ribbons

Directions

Cover shrimp in Creole and jerk seasoning and grill. Heat white sauce in sauté pan and mix in pesto. Toss fettuccini noodles in pesto sauce and garnish with tomatoes and basil.

Submitted by Mark Cotner, owner

Riverside Inn

2629 N. Riverside Road
Ozark, MO 65721
(417) 581-7051

In 1923, Howard Garrison, a young artist and visionary, realized his dream of opening a restaurant. With his father's help, he cleared land along the Finely River an built what was to become the first phase of Riverside Inn.

During Prohibition, Riverside Inn became a noted speakeasy. Bootleg whiskey, slot machines, and dancing made for a lively evening. Mr. Garrison spent some time in jail during this period for "giving the people what they wanted," as he put it.

Riverside Inn's popularity grew throughout the years, so additional rooms were added until it became the 800-seat restaurant it is today. Nearly all of the murals and painting are the works of the late Mr. Garrison.

Tradition is as important as fine food and service. Fried chicken is still a Riverside Inn specialty, as well as the homemade corn fritters that accompany every meal. Howard Garrison's legacy continues as Riverside Inn proudly upholds his vision.

Lobster Thermidor

¼ c. butter
1 c. milk
½ tsp. salt
⅛ tsp. dry mustard
1 tsp. lemon juice
Parmesan cheese

2 Tbsp. flour
2 beaten eggs
⅛ tsp. nutmeg
1 tsp. cooking sherry
4 lobster tails (8 oz.) fully cooked
Paprika

Directions

Cut lobster tails in half and remove meat. Cut meat into bite-size pieces and set aside. In medium saucepan, melt butter and add flour, stirring until smooth. Add milk and cook until thickened, stirring constantly. Remove from heat, add eggs and stir well. Add salt, nutmeg and dry mustard to cooked mixture and stir well. Stir in sherry and lemon juice. Mix sauce with lobster and stuff into lobster shells. Sprinkle with Parmesan cheese and paprika. Bake at 350 degrees until browned.

Submitted by Eric Engel

Italian Restaurant & Market

Historic Downtown Branson
120 N. Sycamore St.
Branson, MO 65616
B(417) 335-4765

Branson's original Italian Restaurant featuring recipes from "The Hill" in St. Louis. Located adjacent to "The Landing" in historic downtown Branson.

Veal Cutlets

2 veal cutlets, pounded
1 c. flour
2 Tbsp. real butter
½ tsp. capers
1 tsp. fresh parsley, chopped

2 Tbsp. salt
Salt & pepper to taste
½ lemon, juiced
Boil eggs, chopped

Directions

Heat skillet over medium heat, add oil. Salt, pepper and flour the veal on both sides, shake off excess. When oil is hot, add veal to pan and lightly brown on both sides. Set veal on warm plate in oven. Melt butter in pan and add lemon juice and capers scraping the bottom of pan. Pour this sauce over the veal and garnish with chopped egg and parsley.

Submitted by Rocky Barnes, owner

SMOKEY BONES BARBEQUE & GRILL

2040 E. Independence St.
Springfield, MO 65804
(417) 890-1945

Resembling a rustic mountain lodge, Smokey Bones Barbeque & Grill serves award-winning barbeque and a broad variety of other American favorites. Its menu features slow-smoked Baby-Back and St. Louis-style ribs, hand-pulled pork, sliced beef brisket, choice steaks, grilled chicken and fish, fresh salads, sandwiches, Buffalo burgers and Angus burgers. Some appetizers and side offerings include Barbeque Chicken Nachos, Old-Fashioned Skillet Corn Bread with crushed pecan butter, green beans and cinnamon apples. Guests also enjoy the restaurant's signature dessert – a bag of fresh "made-to-order" hot cinnamon-sugar doughnuts served with strawberry dipping sauce.

Portobello Chicken

4 boneless skinless chicken breasts (approx. 6-8 oz. each)
Portobello caps (recipe below)　　　　Spinach artichoke stuffing (recipe below)
Salt and pepper to taste　　　　　　　¼ c. diced tomatoes

Portobello Caps & Spinach Artichoke Stuffing

Portobello Cap Ingredients:
4 large Portobello mushroom caps　　　2 Tbsp. vegetable oil
Kosher salt to taste　　　　　　　　　Cracked black pepper to taste

Spinach Artichoke Stuffing Ingredients:
1 box frozen spinach, thawed　　　　　1 c. sour cream
1 c. grated Swiss cheese　　　　　　　8 oz. pkg. cream cheese, softened
¼ tsp. white pepper　　　　　　　　　½ tsp. red pepper flakes
1 tsp. crushed garlic　　　　　　　　　1 can (14 oz.) artichoke hearts, drained
4 oz. feta cheese crumbs

Preparation (at least 4 hours before serving)

Preheat oven to 350° F. While oven is preheating, remove any remaining stem from Portobello caps, then lightly brush any dirt from caps using a dry towel. Place caps on a baking pan, cap side up. Lightly brush each cap with ½ Tbsp. vegetable oil, then sprinkle each evenly with kosher salt and cracked black pepper. Flip caps over to the rib side, and without oiling the cap, sprinkle each evenly with kosher salt and cracked black pepper. With the seasoned caps still rib side up, place the pan in the oven and set timer for 15 minutes. When caps are done, remove from oven and cool 5 minutes at room temperature, then place in refrigerator to chill.

Recipe continued on next page

86

SMOKEY BONES BARBEQUE & GRILL

Portobello Chicken...continued

Preparation (to be done while caps are chilling)

Squeeze water from thawed spinach, then chop into approximate ½ x ½-in. pieces and place into large mixing bowl. Chop artichoke hearts into approximate ½ x ½-in. pieces and add to mixing bowl. Add sour cream, Swiss cheese, cream cheese, white pepper, red pepper flakes and garlic to spinach and artichoke hearts, then mix thoroughly.

Remove chilled Portobello caps from refrigerator and top each with approximately ¼ of spinach artichoke stuffing, spreading evenly to edge of cap. Place 1 oz. of feta cheese crumbles on each cap, spreading evenly to edge of cap. Place in refrigerator until ready for grilling chicken.

Grilling and Completing the Dish

Preheat gas or charcoal grill to medium-high heat. Season chicken breasts with salt and pepper and place on pre-heated grill. With the chicken grilling on medium-high heat, place the stuffed Portobello caps with the cheese side up on a section of the grill set on low heat. Cover caps with aluminum pan.

Cook chicken approximately 4-5 minutes per side, rotating once per side to create diamond marks. Cook until internal temperature reaches 165° F.

Without flipping, rotate stuffed Portobello caps once during cooking to heat evenly. Remove caps to plate when heated completely through and cheese begins to melt slightly. Place one grilled chicken breast on each cap, leaving top half of cap exposed. Top each with 1 tablespoon of diced tomatoes.

Submitted by Smokey Bones Team

ST. JAMES WINERY

540 Sidney St.
St. James, MO 65559
(800) 280-9463
www.StJamesWinery.com

St. James Winery is owned and operated by the Hofherr Family since 1970, conveniently located on Interstate 44, on Old Historic Route 66 only ninety miles southwest of St. Louis, Missouri in St. James, Missouri .

With over 700 miles of vines in Missouri, Arkansas, and Michigan, no other winery in the Eastern United states utilizes such state of the art technology from the vineyards to the bottling room bringing you consistent quality vintages for your enjoyment. With over 1,800 medals to date, no wonder St. James Winery is "America's Midwest Winery". In our area, be sure to stop by our tasting room and sample our wide variety of vintages, our extensive gift shop, and take a tour of our cellars. St. James Winery products are presently distributed in six states and available on our website.

Apricot Pineapple Chicken

1 c. St. James Winery Apricot Pineapple
  Preserves
1 Tbsp. lemon juice
Olive oil

1 c. St. James Seyval Wine
1 Tbsp. corn starch
Salt and pepper to taste
Chicken breasts

Directions

Wash and pat dry chicken breasts. Brown in oil. Salt and pepper to taste. Set aside.

In a saucepan boil preserves and wine together for five minutes. Dissolve the cornstarch in a small amount of cold water and add mixture to the boiling preserves and wine. Boil 5 minutes.

Remove from heat. Add lemon juice and stir.

Pour a small amount of sauce in the bottom of a baking pan. Place chicken on top of sauce and pour the remainder of the sauce over the chicken. Bake at 350 degrees for 20 minutes. Serve over rice. Serves 4.

Submitted by Jack Bonar

12501 Hwy. 13
Kimberling City, MO
(417) 739-4341

Featuring oysters on the half-shell, seafood, steaks, pasta, burgers and more. Just a short drive from Branson and Springfield, Overlooking Tablerock Lake. Featuring The Outdoor Tiki Bar with pool and live music in season.

Ted and Beth's Pasta

6 oz. chicken breast, diced
½ c. fresh mushrooms
½ c. fresh tomatoes
Salt and pepper
½ c. white wine

6-8 jumbo shrimp
½ c. artichoke hearts
Fresh basil
Virgin olive oil

Directions

Sautee chicken and shrimp in olive oil, add mushrooms, artichoke hearts, tomatoes, basil and salt and pepper. Add white wine simmer for a couple of minutes for a nice reduction then pour over your favorite pasta.

Submitted by Beth Whitaker

**2325 Bittersweet
(7 mm by water)
Lake Ozark, MO 65049
(573) 365-5500**

"No entertainment or dining experience comes close!" Having German parents, this is the food I grew up on and has also become one of my wife's favorite dishes at home. Suggested side dishes are fried potatoes and onions or smashed potatoes with gravy. The Horny Toad Restaurant is located on level 3 of the complex offering fine dining in a casual atmosphere.

Weiner Schnitzel & Red Cabbage for Two

Schnitzel:
  4 2-oz. medallions of pork loin
  Flour
  Bread crumbs

  Salt and white pepper
  Egg wash

Red Cabbage:
  1 med. head red cabbage, shredded
  2 apples (Jonathan or Red Delicious)
    peeled and diced
  2 c. brown sugar

  1 med. white onion, diced
  1 tsp. ground clove
  12 oz. red wine vinegar
  Salt and white pepper to taste

Directions

Schnitzel: Pound pork evenly, season with salt and white pepper. Bread (in order) flour, egg wash and bread crumbs. Lightly sauté in butter.

Red Cabbage: Lightly sauté onion in butter. Add cabbage, stir 2-3 minutes then add remaining ingredients and cover with cold water. Bring to a boil, reduce heat, partially cover with lid and simmer 2 hours.

Submitted by Stefan Haney, executive chef

THE PLANTATION

**STEAKS   SEA FOOD
PAN FRIED CHICKEN**

3460 W. Hwy. 76
Branson, MO 65616
(417) 334-7800

Voted the number one restaurant three years in a row by the Ozark Mountain Country Visitor. Delicious breakfast, lunch and dinner buffet with soft-serve ice cream or full-menu service available. Daily features plus steaks, seafood, pan-fried chicken, fresh-water catfish and BBQ ribs. Breakfast: 7-11 a.m., Lunch: 11 a.m. - 4:00 p.m., Dinner: 4:00 p.m.-'til. Buses welcome.

Grilled Chicken Alfredo Pasta

6 oz. grill chicken breast
2 oz. mushrooms
2 oz. Mozzarella cheese
6 oz. white wine cream sauce
2 oz. olive oil
1 oz. scallions

2 oz. bacon
2 oz. red onions (French slice)
1 oz. garlic
7 oz. short pasta
2 oz. Parmesan cheese

Directions

Heat the pan with oil, add the onions, bacon mushrooms, garlic, deglaze with white wine, add the white wine cream sauce, add the Mozzarella cheese, saute, drop the pasta in the water, drain well, add to pan, saute, place into bowl, cut chicken breast up, place on top, garnish with Parmesan and scallions.

Submitted by Plantation staff

THE TOWER CLUB

Twenty-First and Twenty-Second Floors
Atop The Hammons Tower
901 Saint Louis Street
Springfield, MO 65805
(417) 866-4466

The Tower Club is an exclusive town club located in the heart of activity in downtown Springfield. Private parties, luncheons, dinner receptions and meetings for up to 400 people can be accommodated in five private suites, the Starlight Room, or the Main Dining Room. The Tower Club offers panoramic views of the city, superior cuisine, excellent service and the most exquisite dining venue in the city.

Seared Barbecue Rub Pork Tenderloin and Red Bell Pepper Cream with Pork Sausage Mashed Potatoes

12 - 1½ oz. pork tenderloin medallions

Barbecue Rub:

2 Tbsp. fresh garlic
2 Tbsp. black pepper
2 Tbsp. cumin
1 Tbsp. sugar
1 Tbsp. celery salt

3 Tbsp. paprika
2 Tbsp. chili powder
2 Tbsp. brown sugar
1 Tbsp. oregano
1 Tbsp. salt

Mix all ingredients together except garlic.

Directions

Rub both sides of medallions with garlic and then rub both sides with barbecue rub. In an iron skillet on high heat, sear both sides of medallions. Put on lightly greased sheet pan and finish in 350° oven to desired temperature.

Recipe continued on next page

Seared Barbecue Rub Pork Tenderloin...continued

Red Bell Pepper Cream

1 Tbsp. olive oil
1½ oz. Sherry
1 c. roasted red peppers (puréed)
¼ tsp. white pepper

2 Tbsp. shallots (chop fine)
1 c. whipping cream
½ tsp. salt
1 Tbsp. butter

Directions

On high heat, sauté shallots in oil for 1 minute. Deglaze pan with sherry. Add cream, roasted peppers, white pepper and salt. Turn heat off. Swirl in butter. Strain.

Pork Sausage Mashed Potatoes

2 lbs. potatoes (peeled)
1 egg white
½ c. whole milk
3 Tbsp. sour cream
2 Tbsp. roasted garlic, chop fine
½ tsp. white pepper

1½ c. ground pork sausage
   (cooked and drained)
2 Tbsp. butter, softened
1 Tbsp. parsley, chop fine
2 tsp. salt

Directions

Boil or steam potatoes until done (very soft). In a mixing bowl, add potatoes to remaining ingredients, and mix on medium speed for 3-4 minutes. Using a pastry bag, pipe potatoes to desired shape. Heat in oven uncovered until lightly brown.

Submitted by Chef Brad Lyon, C.E.C.

TOP OF THE ROCK RESTAURANT

Big Cedar Lodge Resort
612 Devil's Pool Rd.
Ridgedale, MO 65739
(417) 339-5320
www.big-cedar.com

A unique atmosphere marked by vaulted ceilings, bronze statuary, warm colors and Native American artifacts set the stage for a truly memorable dining experience. Choose from an array of wood-grilled items including steak and Atlantic salmon, Jerk Chicken or try our Signature Rotisserie Chicken, fresh pastas and wood-fired pizzas followed by one of our sumptuous desserts. Incredible dining and The Grandest View in the Ozarks make every meal a special occasion.

Grilled Portabellas over Jalapeno Grits with Red Pepper Coulis

Marinade:
½ c. Balsamic vinegar
2 lbs. chopped fresh thyme
1 c. olive oil
1 Tbsp. chopped garlic

Jalapeno Grits:
1 c. heavy cream
1 c. diced mixed pepper (red, yellow, green)
2 Tbsp. butter
2 Tbsp. diced jalapeno peppers
2½ c. chicken stock/broth
1 c. instant grits
½ lb. pepperjack cheese

Directions

Bring cream and chicken stock to a boil. Slowly add grits and cook for 5-6 minutes. Once grits are cooked, add peppers, jalapenos, butter and cheese. Cover and turn off the heat until all has incorporated.

Marinate mushrooms for 4 hours. Place on a hot grill or in oven for 5-8 minutes. Roast 5 red bell peppers until skin blisters. Place in a pan and cover. Wait 15 minutes and peel the skin and deseed. Place in a sauce pan with ½ c. white wine and 2 shallots. Once wine has reduced, place in food processor and blend until liquid. Place grits on a plate. Slice the portabella on top of the grits and finish with the coulis.

Submitted by Todd Leonard, asst. food and beverage director

TOUCH RESTAURANT

1620 E. Republic Rd.
Springfield, MO
(417) 823-8383

Touch is a beautiful restaurant with an American menu and a touch of Mediterranean. Belly dancing is featured on Thursday, Friday and Saturday nights. Featured entrees are Sea bass and Halibut. Desserts include chocolate torte and Bailey's Irish Cream Cheesecake.

Touch-Sea Bass

8 oz. fresh sea bass	1½ oz. pistachio nuts
1½ oz. English walnuts	2 oz. brown sugar
(mix the nuts with brown sugar in blender)	
2 Tbsp. olive oil	1 lime
(add to above mix)	

Directions

Preheat oven to 350° for 10 minutes. Add mix nuts on top of the sea bass filet and place on baking sheet in middle shelf for 7 minutes. To brown the mix of nuts, move to top shelf for 3 minutes.

Apricot Jam:
¼ c. red onion-julianne cut   ¼ c. dry apricots
¼ c. red wine
Put all in a sauté pan and cook for 15 minutes. Add to top of fish.

Risotto Rice:
½ c. rice   1½ c. chicken broth
1 small shallot, minced and sauté with 3 Tbsp. olive oil then add rice to it. Mix together then add chicken broth and boil for about 7 minutes. Stir as you go. Turn heat off and let set for 5 minutes.

Seafood Lobster Mix:
1 c. heavy cream   1 Tbsp. lobster base
Add together with white pepper, onion powder, garlic powder (1 tsp. each) Squeeze 1 lemon. Bring to boil and then add Tbsp. of corn starch and whisk for thicken sauce. Then add to your risotto rice.

Submitted by Mike Jalili, owner

UNDERCLIFF GRILL & BAR

6385 Old Highway 71
Joplin, MO 64804
(417) 623-8382
www.undercliff.com

The Undercilff Grill & Bar is nestled into the side of a cliff serving locals and tourists alike. The atmosphere is comfortable and the food is wonderful. You can kick back and enjoy our decor, mostly supplied by the locals. Our guests love to bring in friends and family because they feel that it is a home away from home.

Lemon Pepper Chicken Breast

Seasoning slat
Lemon Juice

Pepper
Boneless Chicken Breast

Directions

Generously season one side of the chicken breast with seasoning salt and pepper, and the second side with seasoning salt only. Cook on a flat grill or a skillet, and squirt with lemon juice and pepper. Turning as needed. You will have a juicy tender chicken breast to use as a sandwich, serve over rice, cut up and put on a salad, use for a nacho, or put in a wrap. We use this item in so many of our menu selections. It is very versatile and great no matter how you serve it.

Submitted by Melissa Winn, owner

Discover Uncharted Waterfront Shopping and Dining

It's what you've been waiting for... discover the new Branson Landing located on the waterfront of beautiful Lake Taneycomo, where the adventurous will shop, dine and play!

Stroll the promenade of magnificent shopping with first-to-Branson national retailers including Bass Pro Shops, Belk Department Store, Coldwater Creek, Chicos, Build-A-Bear Workshop, Charlotte Russe, Hollister, White House/Black Market and many more. Enjoy a relaxing lunch or dinner at one of our full-service restaurants along the boardwalk or pick up a quick bite to go.

Add a splash of entertainment with a visit to the Branson Landing Town Square where you will be dazzled by our $7.5 million water spectacular that synchronizes light, sound, music and fire.

Where the Adventurous Shop, Dine & Play

Belk Department Store, Bass Pro Shops
Over 100 specialty stores and restaurants.
Located on Branson Landing Boulevard next to historic Downtown Branson.

www.bransonlanding.com

VALENTINE'S RESTAURANT

2902-B South Campbell
Springfield, MO, 65807
(417) 891-9700
www.valentinesrestaurant.com

STEAKS • PASTA • SEAFOOD

Casual dining at its finest, in an elegant, sophisticated, yet contemporary casual setting. Menu offers hand cut steaks, pasta, seafood, salads, sandwiches & lunch menu. Sunday brunch, full liquor, beer & wine, outside patio seating, happy hour daily 4 p.m.-7 p.m., late night happy hour 9 p.m.-close. Lunch & Dinner, 7 Days. Reservations welcome.

Chesapeake Halibut

7 8-oz. halibut fillets
4 c. shredded cheddar cheese
2 lemons, wedged

4 c. Saltine crackers (approx. 2 sleeves)
4 sticks margarine, slightly melted

Directions

In the food processor or blender, crush the saltine crackers to a medium consistency, approx. 1 minute. In a large stainless steel bowl mix equal parts crackers and cheddar cheese. Dip Halibut in the butter blend and place in the cracker/cheddar mixture. Make sure the entire fillet is coated with an even coating.

Apply non-stick spray to a baking sheet tray before placing fillets on tray. Bake the halibut fillets in the oven at 400° for 12-15 minutes or until breading is golden brown. Garnish with lemon wedge. Serve with potato or rice and a fresh vegetable. Makes 7 servings.

Submitted by Joseph Sunseri, owner

WIMPY'S RESTAURANT

Wee Willy's *Huntin' & Fishin'*

Wimpy's *Restaurant*

Jct. Hwys. 160 & 123, Willard, MO

8374 W. Farm Road 68
Willard, MO 65781
(417) 742-3909

Wimpy's is a family owned and operated business in operation since 1995. Wimpy's serves a wide range of food, from homestyle burgers and home-smoked BBQ to "All-U-Can Eat" shrimp and a multitude of other home-cooked meals. We are "The Home of the 1pound Burger." Wimpy's is conveniently located on the west side of Willard at the junction of highways 160 & 123, just 8 miles northwest of Springfield on Hwy 160. The family also owns & operates a Conoco gas station called The Corner Store, along with a bait & tackle shop called Wee Willy's Huntin' & Fishin', all located on the same property.

Beef Tips

1 lb. sirloin steak
1 Tbsp. onion powder
2 Tbsp. coarse ground pepper
1 green pepper

½ c. soy sauce
1 Tbsp. garlic salt
1 onion

Directions

Chop sirloin into 1" cubes. In large mixing bowl, add sirloin, soy sauce, onion powder, garlic & pepper. With hands, squeeze ingredients into tips. Chop onion & green pepper. Sauté tips with onion and green pepper to desired doneness. Approx. 4 servings.

Oven Roasted Potatoes

15 baking potatoes
2 c. melted margarine
Onion powder

2 1-oz. pkgs. ranch dressing mix
Season salt
Black pepper

Directions

Bake potatoes in oven uncovered until soft. Let cool. Chop potatoes into 1" cubes and put in large mixing bowl. Add melted margarine and stir. Add ranch dressing mix and stir. Add season salt, onion powder and black pepper to taste and stir. Bake in 425° oven approx. 20 min.

Submitted by Bill & Michelle Albert, owners

WHIPPER SNAPPERS RESTAURANT

236 Shepherd of the Hills
Branson, MO 65616
(800) 363-9880

Whipper Snappers Restaurant is the place to go for all-you-can-eat lobster and seafood. The dinner buffet from 4 p.m. to 8 p.m. every night is brimming with fresh, whole lobster, crab legs, crawfish, gumbo, shrimp, clam strips, baked fish and much more! A full menu is also available with a variety of entrees . Open 7 days a week. Located at Hwy. 248 & Shepherd of the Hills Expwy. on Shepherd of the Hills Expwy.

Grilled Salmon w/Roasted Corn
& Asparagus Salsa with a Raspberry Balsamic Drizzle

7 oz. salmon
1 oz. raspberry drizzle

2 oz. roasted corn, asp salsa

Directions

Grill the salmon to the required temperature, place on a plate with salsa on top and drizzle balsamic on top.

Roasted Corn and Asparagus Salsa

2 bunches asparagus
2 white onions, diced small
2 green peppers, diced small
¼ c. balsamic vinegar

4 c. corn
2 red peppers, diced small
½ c. cilantro, chopped

Grill the asparagus and roast the corn off, leave to cool, then add to the rest of the vegetables.

Raspberry Balsamic Drizzle

2 c. frozen raspberries
1 c. balsamic reserve

1 c. sugar

Boil the raspberries with the sugar until raspberries are cooked, then add balsamic reserve, boil until desired consistency, strain.

Submitted by Whipper Snapper staff

WHITE RIVER FISH COMPANY

Located at Bass Pro Shops
The Branson Landing
Branson, Missouri
COMING SOON

The 11,255 sq. ft. floating White River Fish Company restaurant is part of the all new Bass Pro Shops retail store in Branson, MO. Located at the Branson Landing development adjacent to historic downtown and Lake Taneycomo. In addition to the floating restaurant other features of the Branson location will include an approximate 68-slip operating marina, guide service, boat rental and boat service center. The Bass Pro Shops store is tentatively scheduled to open in June.

Grouper Sicily

4 portions grouper fillets (8-10 oz. ea.)
1 lb. Japanese style bread crumbs.
12 oz. sliced fresh mushrooms
2 oz. chopped fresh garlic
2 oz. white wine (Chablis is great)

6 oz ranch dressing
4 oz. clarified margarine (see recipe)
1 bunch scallions, cleaned and sliced
2 oz. unsalted butter

Directions

Bring to boil in a small saucepan one lb. of margarine. Allow to boil 10 minutes, then let sit. The clear yellow liquid that rises to the top is clarified margarine, and is great for cooking fish.

Clean and rinse fish fillets. Roll in ranch dressing, then in Japanese bread crumbs. The ranch dressing will stick to the fish, and the bread crumbs to the ranch dressing, "breading" the fish.

In a hot non-stick skillet, place the clarified margarine, then the breaded grouper fillets. Cook until golden brown, and turn. Allow to cook 2-3 minutes, then remove from the skillet and place on an ungreased cookie sheet. Place in a 350° oven, for approximately 10 minutes or until the fish is completely cooked.

Wipe the skillet clean, and place the mushrooms, garlic, and white wine. Allow to cook 1-2 minutes, until the mushrooms are soft. Add the scallions and butter. Allow to heat only until the butter is melted. DO NOT OVERCOOK.

Remove the fish from the oven. Place on 4 serving plates, and top with 1/4 of the mushroom/scallion/garlic butter mixture.

Serve with pride. This dish is great with some zucchini provencale or some pasta.

Submitted by Steven Todd, general manager

the
WORMAN
H O U S E

612 Devil's Pool Road
Ridgedale, MO 65739
(417) 335-2777

A former country retreat for Frisco Railroad executive Harry Worman, this elegant setting is home to our elaborate Champagne Sunday Brunch. No effort is spared to bring you the finest in culinary offerings amid luxurious surroundings. Our Sunday brunch features fresh fruits and breakfast breads, salads and charcuterie, delicious hot entrees, omelettes cooked to order and Belgian waffles, freshly carved meats and delectable desserts. Some traditional favorites are served weekly, while our chefs prepare a variety of special offerings each Sunday.

Grilled Salmon with Jacama and Cucumber Slaw With a Champagne Dill Compound Butter

1 cucumber	1 med. size jacama
1 Tbsp. rice wine vinegar	Salt and pepper to taste

Deseed and slice the cucumber and jacama. Add to rice wine vinegar, slat and pepper and marinate for 1 hour.

1 c. champagne	2 peppercorns
1 bay leaf	½ lb. butter
⅛ c. cream	

Reduce all ingredients in a small sauce pan by one-half. Add cream and bring back to a boil. take off heat and slowly whisk in the butter, strain and set aside. Grill the salmon for 4 minutes on each side, or to a medium rare. Place slaw on plate on top and finish with sauce.

Submitted by Todd Leonard, asst. food and beverage director

ZIGGIE'S CAFE

Ziggie's Cafe

Breakfast Anytime

All Ziggie's Cafe locations phone number:
(417) 883-0900
www.ziggiescafe.com

5 LOCATIONS:

2222 South Campbell Ave.
Springfield, MO – 24 Hours

853 North Glenstone Ave.
Springfield, MO– 24 Hours

1324 West Kearny St.
Springfield, MO – 5 a.m. - 11 p.m.

901 North Kenneth
Nixa, MO – 6 a.m.-10 p.m.

1230 West Hwy. 80
Republic, MO – 6 a.m. - 10 p.m.

Ziggie's Café is a 24 hour family owned and operated restaurant that specializes in friendly service. We have been serving the Springfield area for over 20 years. We take pride in our loyal customers and the service that we provide for them. Our goals are to provide a friendly atmosphere, fast service, and great food, 7 days a week.

Our menu is one of the largest in the city; offering breakfast served anytime, as well as sandwiches, pastas, steaks, and desserts.

We also offer take out dining and provide full catering service. (417) 881-5154

Gift cards are available to purchase and may be used at any location.

Fresh Spinach & Mozzarella Chicken

8 oz. chicken breast
⅛ c. shredded Mozzarella cheese
Aluminum foil

8 fresh spinach leaves
Salt and pepper

Directions

Roll spinach and Mozzarella cheese in chicken breast. Salt and pepper to taste. Wrap in aluminum foil. Place in boiling water for 15 minutes or until chicken is thoroughly cooked.

1½ oz. (45 gm) butter
2 cloves garlic, crushed
Salt and pepper
½ pt. (280 ml) milk

1 onion, finely chopped
1 glass dry white wine
1 oz. (30 gm) flour

Melt ½ oz. (15 gm) butter in a pan, add the chopped onions and cook gently until soft and golden. Add the garlic and cook for another minute or so. Season with salt and pepper to taste. Add the wine, turn up the heat and reduce the volume by about half. Remove from heat.

Now add milk, slowly. Stir, then add a little more. When it resembles an elastic dough beat it smooth. Add the rest of the milk and keep stirring. You'll end up with a nice thick sauce. Mix in the onion and garlic and you're done. Serve the garlic sauce warm. If things go wrong and the garlic sauce is lumpy just bung it in a food processor and whizz for a few seconds.

Submitted by Ziggie's staff

★★★★★ RESTAURANT

Recipes of

MISCELLANEOUS

AGRARIO RESTAURANT

311 S. Patton
Springfield, MO 65806
(417) 865-4255
www.agrariorestaurant.com

Agrario is an upscale contemporary restaurant in the heart of Downtown Springfield, Mo. Housed in a restored livery stable built in 1860, we stayed true to the original architecture while creating a comfortable modern restaurant. We have two major influences when it comes to food. First we use as much local product as possible. This allows us to be sure that our ingredients are as fresh and flavorful as possible. We combine these local ingredients with influences from the entire Mediterranean region (Spain all the way to North Africa) to create contemporary dishes that represent various seasons. For this reason we change our menus seasonally to best represent the products that we are receiving from our farmers.

Creamy Zucchini with Gorgonzola

2 Tbsp. olive oil
1 yellow onion, roughly chopped
6 c. sliced zucchini
2½ c. vegetable stock
Garnish: springs of fresh oregano, crumbled Gorgonzola

1 Tbsp. butter
Salt and freshly ground pepper
1 tsp. dried oregano
4 oz. Gorgonzola, crumbled

Directions

Heat oil and butter in a large saucepan until foaming. Add the onion and cook slowly for about 5 minutes, stirring frequently until soft but not brown. Add the zucchini and oregano with salt and pepper to taste. Cook over medium heat for 10 minutes stirring frequently. Pour in the stock and bring to a boil stirring frequently. Lower the heat, half-cover the pan and simmer stirring occasionally for about 30 minutes. Stir in Gorgonzola to melt. Blend until smooth and strain. Add ⅔ of cream and stir. Do not boil. Adjust seasoning. Serve in warm bowls and garnish with a swirl of remaining cream, fresh oregano and Gorgonzola crumbles.

Submitted by John Gray, chef

1622 Horseshoe Bend Pkwy.
Lake Ozark, MO 65049
(573) 365-2800

Andre's Restaurant - an inviting restaurant situated atop a bluff overlooking The Lake of the Ozarks, provides diners a change from the Ordinary. It is located on Horseshoebend Parkway, close to resorts and hotels The owner Andre Torres, a certified executive chef, oversees the daily operation. Andre's food transports diners around a world of culinary delights-steaks grilled on a woodfire grill, lobster with a champagne butter, chicken, fish, veal, and pasta. Inside Andre's, make sure you have a martini at Le Fou Bar - (a great bar with a vast martini list, specialty drinks, and a light bar menu) During summer do not miss Sunday Brunch from 9:00AM-1:00PM. Cooking classes September to May at 6:00 PM International night every third Friday of the Month.

Potato & Wild Mushroom Strudel

2 large baking potatoes
1 c. fine diced onion
3 c. wild mushrooms
2 Tbsp. white wine (can use vermouth)
2 Tbsp. chopped fresh thyme
Kosher salt and black pepper to taste
½ c. clarified butter

3 Tbsp. olive oil
1 clove garlic, minced
½ c. goat cheese
2 Tbsp. chopped sage
2 Tbsp. chopped fresh parsley
2 sheet phyllo dough

Directions

Preheat oven to 400° F. In a large pot of salted water, cook the potatoes until just done. Cool the potatoes slightly, peel them and cut into small dice. Place the potatoes in a medium mixing bowl.

In a large skillet put the olive oil and sautee the onion and garlic until soft. Then add the mushrooms. When the mushrooms are cooked add the herbs and the white wine. Pour the mushroom mixture onto the potatoes and mix.

Lay one sheet of the phyllo dough out on a table and brush with clarified butter. Repeat 1 more times. Place the potato mixture on the ⅓ of the buttered phyllo dough and roll into a tight cylinder.

Brush the outside of the strudel with the butter and refrigerate for 30 minutes. Bake at 400° F for 15 minutes and then reduce the heat to 350° and bake for another 15 minutes. Cut the strudel in 6 slices and serve on a small salad with a light vinaigrette.

Submitted Andre Torres, owner and executive chef

BIERMANN'S GENERAL STORE RESTAURANT

**226 N. Main St.
Freistatt, MO 65798
(417) 235-9005
www.biermannsfinedining.com**

In 1962, after 78 years of successful enterprising in Freistatt, the doors of Biermann's General Store closed. In 1979 the building was purchased from the grandchildren of H. Biermann and remodeling began for Biermann's General Store Restaurant. The primary goal of the owner, Deena Bottom, was to maintain and restore as much of the General Store as possible. German cuisine was served and Biermann's became a well known and successful restaurant for over 20 years. 2003! New owner and operator Ansel Jay Sitton asks that you dine leisurely and sense the Gemulichkeit, but most importantly enjoy the food we are about to serve you. If you are planning a private banquet, meeting or luncheon, we have facilities to accommodate groups from 20 to 100.

Potato Pancakes (Kartoffelpuffer)

2 lbs. peeled potatoes, boiled
1 tsp. ea. salt, pepper, granulated garlic
¼ cup diced bacon
2 c. shredded hash browns

1 egg
¼ c. diced cucumber
¼ c. flour
Oil for frying pan

Directions

Mash potatoes and mix all ingredients until distributed evenly. Form two ounce patties and fry until golden brown. Tip: add milk if too thick, or add another egg or more flour if too thin.

Submitted by Jay Sitton, owner

Boardwalk Grill

401 N. Main
Laurie, MO 65038
(573) 374-6002

The Boardwalk Grill is a relaxed and casual seafood and steak house located in Laurie, Missouri. Steve and Nick Stock (owner/general manager) constructed the Boardwalk Grill in the spring of 2004. Operations began in early August of 2004. Open All Year at 11:00 a.m., Monday - Saturday. We hope that you enjoy a few of our favorite dishes!

Cajun Shrimp

½ c. olive oil
2 Tbsp. lemon juice
1 Tbsp. honey
Pinch cayenne pepper

2 Tbsp. Cajun seasoning
2 Tbsp. fresh parsley, chopped
1 Tbsp. soy sauce
1 lb. shrimp, uncooked, shelled, deveined

Directions

Combine first seven ingredients in a 9" x 13" baking dish. Add shrimp and toss to coat. Refrigerate at least 1 hour. Preheat oven to 450 degrees. Bake until shrimp are cooking through, stirring occasionally, about 10 minutes. I sometimes serve with fettucini alfredo and French bread.

Submitted by Nicholas Stock, general manager

BRUNO'S RESTAURANT

Fine Italian Casual Dining

416 South Ave.
Springfield, MO 65806
(417) 866-0007
www.brunos-restaurant.net

Bruno Gargiulo brings tastes of his Italian home to downtown Springfield. He is making authentic Italian cuisine with the best ingredients he can find. His specialty is Southern Italian cooking. Gargiulo makes almost everything on-site. He and his wife Melissa spend each morning preparing dough for their bread and pizza crusts. "Everything is special on the menu because you won't find it anywhere else," he said. More than 60 Italian wines representing different regions of Italy are offered at Bruno's.

Involtini di Pesce Spada
(Swordfish Rolls)

2 lbs. swordfish, very thinly sliced and trimmed (about 6 oz. each slice)
Extra virgin olive oil
1 Tbsp. capers
3 oz. bread crumbs
8 oz. swordfish trimmings
2 Tbsp. raisins
Salt and pepper

1 onion, chopped
1 clove garlic, chopped
Parsley, chopped
3 oz. Parmesan or Provolone picante or Pecorino
Few anchovies chopped (optional)
2 Tbsp. pine nuts
2 eggs

Directions

Chop and brown the onion, garlic and bits of the swordfish trimmings in some olive oil. Add the bread crumbs, the capers, the pine nuts, the anchovies, the raisins (after they have been soaked in warm water for 20 minutes) and near the end add the parsley. Cool and pass through a food mill. Combine the grated cheese and the eggs with the mixture, add the salt and pepper to taste, and make a smooth filling (if the mixture feels too dry, add more olive oil). Flatten the swordfish slices slightly with a mallet and place a spoonful of filling in the middle. Roll up the slices and close them with toothpicks. The rolls can be grilled or sautéed in olive oil. Before serving, pour the salmoriglio sauce over the rolls.

Salmoriglio Sauce: extra virgin olive oil, fresh lemon juice, oregano, parsley, chopped garlic, salt and pepper.

Submitted by Bruno Gargiulo, owner

CASPER'S RESTAURANT

601 W. Walnut
Springfield, MO 65804
(417) 866-9750

Casper's is a fun dining experience housed in a quonset hut and known for the famous chili and old-fashioned burgers as well as its unique 1960's hippie like decor with customers as diverse as the unusual cafe itself. Casper's has been in business since 1909 making it the oldest restaurant in Springfield. We are open from 10:30 a.m. til 4:00 p.m. Monday thru Friday and closed during the months of June, July, and August. We re-open every year the day after Labor Day for another season.

About the recipe: Charles Lederer, the previous owner, was an artist who made elaborate Christmas ornaments out of dough every year and hung them over the counter. Although our art work pales in comparison we still do this in honor of Charles and the wonderful tradition of his art and Casper's.

Casper's Christmas Dough Ornaments

4 c. flour   1 c. salt
1½ c. water (add more if dough is too dry)

Directions

Knead dough together till soft and easy to form into shapes and then just use your imagination to free-form whimsical "Christmas Stuff." I like to do weird Santas, funny cross-eyed angels, stars with faces, or whatever! When baking in a 350° oven they puff up and take on a life of their own. Bake till brownish and remember before you put them in the oven to form a hole so you can hang them. Get a group of friends together and get creative but don't try to eat them! This is a time of fun, just like Casper's!

Submitted by Belinda Harriman, owner

COOKIN' FROM SCRATCH

I-44 Exit 179
Doolittle, MO
(573) 762-3111

Located midway between St. Louis and Springfield, MO. Cookin' from Scratch is a favorite stop for the traveler and most importantly, our local clientele. Whether your favorite meal is breakfast, lunch or dinner, we have a unique variety of offering to satisfy the most demanding palette. Our huge iron skillets fry up some of the most delicious chicken anywhere around. It's so good no one has ever tried to copy it, as so many other restaurants try to steal someone else's good idea.

The Lumberjack
(The best omelette in the business)

Hash browns (about 4 oz.)
1 2-oz. sausage pattie, cooked & broken up
2 strips bacon, cooked and crumbled
2 c. sausage gravy

3 eggs beaten
2 oz. diced ham
½ c. shredded cheddar cheese

Directions

Brown hash browns to desired crispness, move aside. Spread egg out on grill in an oval shape. Cook on one side until firm enough to flip. Spread meat out on grill to heat. Flip omelette over. Add meat in a line down the short center. Add about ½ of the cheese spread out on the meat. Fold omelette together. Put hash browns on plate. Put omelette over potatoes. Put gravy over omelette. Sprinkle rest of cheese over all. Enjoy!

Submitted by Tony Sherrer, owner

DEVIL'S POOL RESTAURANT

Big Cedar Lodge Resort
612 Devil's Pool Rd.
Ridgedale, MO 65739
(417) 335-2777
www.big-cedar.com

There is no mystery as to what attracted entrepreneur Jude Simmons to this slice of Ozarks wilderness. The gentle hillsides were an ideal backdrop for his rustic getaway that would reflect the grandeur of Adirondacks lodges and entertain in casual elegance. The home featured native materials, including a huge stone fireplace that still warms our dining room when fall and winter chill the air. Today, hand wrought metal chandeliers cast a warm glow over antique furnishings and our 100 year old mahogany bar. Bark covered logs and exposed rafters are a fitting complement to the sporting gear and animal mounts that adorn our walls in the Bass Pro tradition.

Smoked Trout Cakes

1⅓ lb. whitefish, steamed
¼ red pepper, diced fine
4 green onions, sliced thin
2 oz. Dijon mustard
¾ c. Japanese bread crumbs
¼ tsp. salt

1⅓ lb. smoked trout
¼ green pepper, diced fine
⅛ c. capers
¼ c. mayonnaise
½ Tbsp. old bay seafood seasoning

Directions

Steam and cool whitefish. Place in a large mixing bowl. Add all ingredients and mix thoroughly. Weigh out into 2½ oz. portions, then patty out into 3 inch diameter cake. Sautée trout cakes until golden brown.

Submitted by Todd Leonard, asst. food and beverage director

FAMOUS DAVE'S

New Location
At Branson Landing
Branson, MO
COMING SOON

The recipe is part of a collection of "Down Home" cooking in Dave's fabulous book Famous Dave's Backroads and Sidestreets (proceeds from the book benefit charity). You'll never look at Corn Bread the same way again.

Famous Dave's Corn Bread with Honey Jalapeño Glaze

1 C. yellow cornmeal
1 (9 oz.) package yellow cake mix
1 tsp. salt
½ c. milk
¼ c. vegetable oil
2 Tbsp. light brown sugar
1 Tbsp. mayonnaise

1 C. stone ground cornmeal
2 tsp. baking powder
⅛ tsp. cayenne
½ c. buttermilk
2 eggs, beaten
2 Tbsp. honey

Jalapeño Honey Glaze
½ c. butter
3 Tbsp. red bell pepper, finely diced
⅛ tsp. cayenne

1 large jalapeño pepper, seeded, finely diced
¼ c. honey

Directions

Combine cornmeals, cake mix, baking powder, salt and cayenne in a bowl, set aside.

Combine milk, buttermilk, oil, eggs, brown sugar and honey in a bowl and mix well. Add to the cornmeal mixture and mix gently - there should be no lumps, but do not overmix. Fold in the mayonnaise. Let rest, covered, in the refrigerator for 30 minutes or up to overnight.

Preheat oven to 400° F. Spoon the cold batter into a greased muffin tin or a cast iron skillet. Bake for 25 - 30 minutes or until a cake tester comes out clean and the top is golden brown.

In the meantime, make the glaze by heating butter in a saucepan until melted. Stir in jalapeño and bell pepper. Bring to a simmer. Stir in honey and cayenne. Bring to a simmer, stirring occasionally. Remove from heat. Drizzle over Famous Dave's Corn Bread.

Submitted by Famous Dave

FAT & HAPPY

5806 N. Main St.
Joplin, MO
(417) 626-2002

Fat & Happy was born Nov. 18, 1997 as a Burger & Beverage establishment. Known for our "Great Burgers" – 2 lb. Family Burger, 1 lb. Fat Burger, ½ lb. Pudgie Burger, ¼ lb. Sissy Burger. We also have home made chili and a full line bar and cold beer. Fat & Happy also features an outdoor patio, covered beer hut, horseshoes, basketball and sand volleyball. Owners Gary & Karen Garvin invite you to come and see us.

Fry Bread

2 c. self-rising flour
½ c. sugar

1¼ c. milk
Pinch of salt

Directions

Mix above ingredients until moist. Pat out on a floured surface. ½-inch thick - cut into 3-inch squares. Fry in oil 350° until golden brown.

Indian Corn

1½ lb. pork
2 boxes dried sweet corn

1 lb. beef

Directions

Put beef and pork in large stock pan. Cover with water. Salt and pepper to taste. Boil until tender. Take meat out and pull apart in bite-sized pieces. Put corn and meats back in meat broth. Simmer covered for an hour or so.

Submitted by Karen Garvin, owner

First & Last
Restaurant

Highway 39-S
Shell Knob, MO 65747
(417) 858-4054

The First & Last Restaurant is on the south side of Shell Knob, MO near beautiful Table Rock Lake. The building itself has been everything from a gas station to an awning business and several eating establishments. It has recently been renovated with new hardwood flooring and booths made from 80-year-old church pews and lake decor.

Italian Sausage & Pepper

5 lbs. Italian sausage (links or ring). Poke holes in sausage and boil slowly for 45 minutes to remove fat.

In a separate pan:
1 c. olive oil
2 large onions cut julian
3 tsp. fennel seed
3 tsps. basil
1 tsp. black pepper
¾ c. red wine

⅓ c. minced garlic
3 large or 7 small green peppers,
 cut in squares
½ tsp. salt
½ tsp. crushed red pepper
4 tsp. oregano

Directions

Sauté above items for about 8 minutes stirring frequently. Add sausage (cut to desired bite size) and add 10 cups whole plum tomatoes. Simmer for about 20 minutes until peppers are tender. Serve over pasta or as a sandwich.

Submitted by Joseph & Lydia Macri

GEARHEAD GRILL

12651 Gateway Dr.
Neosho, MO 64850
(417) 455-0506
www.gearheadgrill.com

Created by Mark Eads in January 2002, the Gearhead Grill has unique motorcycle, race car and hot rod decor. Customers come from all walks of life to enjoy a very comfortable and casual dining visit.

Crock Burger

5.3 oz. chopped sirloin
Texas toast
Swiss cheese

Onions, sliced thin
American cheese
Gearhead sauce (call for info)

Directions

Cook sirloin patty, grill onions in butter, add Gearhead sauce, and grilled onions. Melt one slice of American and one slice of Swiss cheese. Serve on buttered Texas toast.

Submitted by Mark Eads

GEM OF "INDIA"

211 W. Battlefield
Springfield, MO 65807
(417) 881-9558

Gem of India has been serving Springfield with fine Indian cuisine for the past 3 years. The chef/owner has worked in fine Indian restaurants in Boston since 1992. We serve authentic Indian cuisine made with the finest and freshest ingredients. We strive to provide excellent service and mouth watering delicacies with enticing ambience. We hope to serve Springfield for a long time to come.

Aloo Gobhi
(Potatoes and cauliflower)

1 cauliflower
¼ c. oil
1 in. stick ginger
¾ tsp. turmeric
3 tomatoes
2 tsp. coriander powder

4 potatoes
1 tsp. cumin seeds
3 cloves of garlic
1 tsp. red chili powder
1 tsp. Garam Masala

Directions

Cut cauliflower into flowerets. Cube potatoes. Heat oil and sauté cumin seeds for about a minute. Add garlic and ginger, stir in potatoes. Bhoona,* add turmeric and chili powder, and bhoona again. Add tomatoes and simmer for about 5 minutes. Add cauliflower and high heat for about a minute. Lower heat, cover and let simmer for about 15 minutes. Curry should be damp-dry.

*Bhoona is a technique that is essential to Indian cooking. The bhoona technique means that the mixture is cooked over medium-high heat, with constant stirring to avoid scorching, until all liquids are reduced and the spices coat the meat like a paste. About ½ cup of water can then be added, the dish covered, and a gravy created as the dish becomes liquefied again. This recipe for Aloo Gobhi serves 4.

Submitted by Gurdev Singh, owner

820 East Walnut
Springfield, MO 65806
(417) 862-6400

Nicola Gilardi began his career in the culinary arts at the family's restaurant in Italy. Upon learning the importance of a strong work ethic, he decided to pursue his dream of owning his own restaurant. "Every customer of mine is not only treasured for the existence of my business but also as a friend. My employees and I strive to provide the best Italian dining experience possible," says Nicola.

"My business thrives on people who are regulars. About ninety percent of our customer base are regulars. The remaining ten percent will be after the first dinner".

Funghi Genovese Con Polenta
(*Sautéed wild mushrooms*)

Polenta:
1½ qts. water
3 Tbsp. butter
2 tsp. salt

13.2 oz. instant polenta
1 c. Parmesan cheese

Directions

Bring water and salt to a boil, add polenta while stirring very rapidly with a wooden spoon or firm whisk. Turn heat to low and cook for 5 minutes, then fold in cheese and butter. It should be a smooth, thick consistency.

Funghi:
2 oz. olive oil
½ lb. white mushroom
1 c. dry white wine

2 cloves garlic, sliced
½ lb. shitakee mushroom
½ Tbsp. lemon juice

Directions

In a large hot skillet put oil and garlic until brown, then add mushrooms. Cook them until they are a nice golden brown, deglaze with white wine and lemon juice.

Submitted by Nicola Gilardi, chef/owner

GREENSIDE BAR & GRILL

At Lake Valley Country Club
Lake Road 54-79
Camdenton, MO 65020
(573) 346-7213

This dish is best served with fish of any type. Greenside Bar & Grill is a simple bar & grill with gourmet food.

Garlic Pomme Puree

2 large boiling potatoes, peeled
6 garlic cloves, unpeeled
White pepper to taste
2½ Tbsp. unsalted butter, cut in slices

Salt as needed
⅔ c. whole milk
¼ c. heavy cream

Directions

Cut potatoes into uniformly size chunks. Cook in heavy salted water until tender (12-15 minutes). Drain well. Return to pan. Place over low heat for 1-2 minutes to dry out. Mash and return to pan.

Blanch garlic clove for 1 minute, drain and refresh in cold water. Repeat 2 more times. Peel and mash into puree. Mix in potatoes.

Scald milk, slowly stir into potatoes with salt and pepper to taste. Slowly add cream. Gradually stir in butter. Serve hot.

Submitted by Chris Wells, food and beverage manager

HK's RESTAURANT

**Lodge of Four Seasons
Golf Resort and Spa Shiki
Horseshoe Bend Parkway
Lake Ozark, MO 65049
(573) 365-3000**

HK's Restaurant, named after Lodge of Four Seasons Founder Harold Koplar, offers fine food in a casual resort setting. Originally located at the Witches Cove golf course, HK's has recently moved to the main Lodge building where our new home boasts spectacular views of the Lake and the Japanese Gardens. Great Steaks, Seafood, Pastas and Gourmet Pizzas are featured on the menu.

Grilled Portabello

4 large portabello mushrooms
2 c. olive oil
4 cloves fresh garlic

1 sprig fresh thyme
4 green peppercorns

2 oz. salted butter
12 oz. fresh spinach

6 oz. Gorgonzola cheese

Directions

Place the mushrooms upside down on a cutting board. Using a paring knife, remove all of the dark underbelly and set it aside. In a deep 1 qt. container, combine the olive oil, fresh garlic (cleaned and minced), fresh thyme and peppercorns. Place the mushrooms in the marinade, making sure that they are all completely immersed in the oil.

Cover and store overnight. (You can begin marinating the mushrooms up to several days in advance).

Remove the Mushrooms from the marinade and pat them dry with a paper towel. Grill over a medium hot grill for about three minutes on each side. Remove from direct heat.

Place the butter in a 10" sauté pan and toss the spinach in the butter over medium heat, until it wilts and takes on a bright green color. Place 3 oz. of the spinach on the center of each serving plate, slice the mushrooms on a bias and arrange them over the spinach. Finally, top the mushroom with the Gorgonzola cheese and melt it under a broiler until it begins to run. Serve and enjoy!

Submitted by Gary Leap, HK's Sous Chef

HEMINGWAY'S BLUE WATER CAFE

Located on the 4th floor of Bass Pro Shops
1935 S. Campbell
Springfield, MO 65898
(417) 891-5100
www.hemingwaysbluewatercafe.com

Hemingway's Blue Water Cafe is a Fantastic place to eat for any occasion. We have a variety of Entrees' for an unforgettable meal. We provide a fine dining experience in a unique casual atmosphere showcasing a 30,000 gallon saltwater tank and numerous exotic displays. Our culinary features include a vast array of seafood and freshwater fish as well as steaks, pork chops, and chicken dishes. A kids menu is also available. In addition to our high quality menu items, we offer a buffet for breakfast, lunch, and dinner Monday through Saturday as well as a brunch buffet on Sundays.

Venison Grand Veneur

24 oz. trimmed venison loin
½ lb. sliced bacon
1 Tbsp. olive oil
Marinade:
  ½ gal. red wine
  Carrots, sliced
  ½ head celery, diced
  1 med. onion, sliced
  1 bunch fresh parsley, chopped

1 Tbsp. butter
½ Tbsp. salt
1 Tbsp. cracked black pepper

1 garlic clove, chopped
3 pinches salt
1 Tbsp. cracked black pepper
2 Tbsp. red wine vinegar

Directions

Salt and pepper the venison loin and soak in the marinade overnight. When ready to cook, wrap the loin with slices of bacon and tie with twine. Strain the marinade and keep vegetables on the side. Heat a large skillet, add olive oil and butter and when the butter turns to a golden grown, sear the loin on all four sides and remove. Sauté the marinated vegetables in the same skillet utilizing the drippins from the loin until light brown. Place the vegetables in a roasting pan.

Add remaining marinade to a sauté pan, bring to a boil and reduce to half. Pour the reduced marinade into the roasting pan with the vegetables. Place venison loin on top of the vegetables. Braise at 375° for 10 minutes. Periodically, baste venison with juices and continue cooking for 5 to 10 minutes or until desired temperature is reached.

Slice the loin and serve with Grand Veneur sauce accompanied with a bouqettiere of fresh vegetables and Shitake and Oyster mushroom sautéed in garlic and olive oil.

Submitted by Chef Marcel Bonetti, CEC, AAC

KIM'S BREADBASKET

614 S. Main Street
Lockwood, MO 65682
(417) 232-4687

Kim's Breadbasket is a local coffee shop in downtown Lockwood Missouri right next to the train track. We have daily specials for breakfast and lunch, Monday thru Friday 6 a.m. to 3 p.m. Saturday 6 a.m. to 2 p.m. We have home cooked meals like chicken fried steak, brisket, fried chicken, pork tenderloin and many more. Our lunch specials consist of meatloaf, Salisbury steak, pork roast and catfish. Stop in and see us for a good home cooked meal and maybe you might even get an education while you're here.

Cinnamon Rolls

2 c. mashed potatoes
¾ c. butter
¼ c. butter, melted
1 c. brown sugar
1 c. sugar
4 tsp. salt

4 c. milk
4 eggs
1 tsp. cinnamon
12 c. flour divided
4 Tbsp. yeast

Directions

Heat potato, milk and butter until warm. In a mixer mix 4 c. flour, sugar, yeast, and salt. Add milk mixture, mix add 4 eggs mix for 5 minutes on medium speed. Put dough hook on mixer and add 8 c. flour. Mix until well kneaded, sometimes I mix for 30 minutes. Turn off mixer and let dough double in size. Roll out on floured surface until dough is about 1 inch thick. Spread with melted butter than sprinkle with cinnamon than cover with brown sugar. Then roll dough up like a jelly roll. Slice in 1 inch pieces and place in a greased cake pan. Makes 2 dozen. Bake on 350° for 20 minutes. Make sure they are done on the bottom or they will fall. Let set for 20 minutes.

Frosting:

6 Tbsp. butter
1½ tsp. vanilla extract

3 c. powdered sugar
2 to 3 Tbsp. milk

Mix butter, powdered sugar, vanilla and milk until the right consistency. Frost warm rolls.

Submitted by Kim Whitesell

LI'L RIZZO'S ITALIAN RESTAURANT

434 Horseshoe Bend
Lake Ozark, MO 65049
(573) 365-3003

929 Chef St.
Osage Beach, MO 65065
(573) 302-1500

Not just pizza and pasta anymore–everything from sandwiches to steaks, gourmet pizza, pasta and "World Famous House Salad" is served at Li'l Rizzo's. There are two locations for your convenience with dine-in or carryout available.

Chicken Spiedini

3 2-oz. raw chicken strips
¼ c. Parmesan cheese
1 oz. chopped garlic
1 tsp. black pepper
Garlic Butter:
  1 oz. butter
  ¼ oz. parsley

1 c. Italian crumbs
1 oz. olive oil
1 tsp. salt
½ tsp. red pepper flakes

½ tsp. garlic

Directions

Combine all ingredients in a container. Let marinate for one hour. Take chicken and put onto skewers. Coat chicken in bread and cook on grill. When chicken is done (7-8 min. each side) put on plate and top with garlic butter. Sprinkle Parmesan cheese and parsley.

Chicken Modiga

1 8-oz. chicken breast
1 c. Italian bread crumbs
1 egg
¼ oz. bacon, chopped
1 oz. mushrooms
Lemon Sauce:
  4 oz. water
  2 oz. white wine
  (thicken with flour and butter mix)

1 tsp. chopped garlic
¼ c. milk
½ c. flour
1 oz. provel cheese
6 oz. lemon sauce

2 tsp. ck paste
1 tsp. lemon juice

Directions

Combine milk and egg. Put chicken breast in flour and milk mixture then into bread crumbs. Cook on grill until done. Combine lemon sauce, mushrooms, bacon and garlic. Cook until boiling. When chicken breast is done, put on plate and top with cheese. Pour lemon sauce over chicken breast.

Submitted by Li'l Rizzo's

MERLE'S HOT DOG EMPORIUM

319½ E. Walnut
Springfield, MO 65806
(417) 862-3902

Merle's Hot Dog Emporium and Sweet Susie's Sweets is quickly becoming a downtown dining hotspot! Try one of Merle's all-beef Kosher hot dogs with a huge variety of toppings! Try a Chicago Dog, a Downtown Dog, A Frito Pie, a wrap, or the best chicken salad in town! Merle's also serves breakfast with excellent biscuits and gravy, or a world-famous Susie's Slinger. Sweet Susie's Sweets offers 187 different types of award-winning cheesecakes, many of which are served at restaurants all over town. Try the Gooey Butter Cake or a slice of Red Velvet Cake. For bigger events, ask about full-service catering.

Susie's Slinger

Hash browns
Sausage gravy
Cheddar cheese, shredded

Scrambled eggs
Chili

Directions

While hash browns are frying, scramble eggs. Place hash browns on plate, top with remaining ingredients in the following order: scrambled eggs, chili, sausage gravy, sprinkle cheddar cheese over all.

Sausage Bites

1 roll sausage, scrambled & drained
1 box Stove Top stuffing
¾ c. cranberry sauce

1 egg
1¾ c. water
Melted butter

Directions

Mix all ingredients together except melted butter. Roll into balls and place on aluminum foil lined baking sheet. Brush each with melted butter. Bake in 350° oven for 20 minutes.

Submitted by Susie & Gerald Wolfe

298 E. 19th St.
Mountain Grove, MO 65711
(417) 926-0113

Mike's Bar-BQ is decorated western style with a combination of western pictures and antiques collected from the Family Farm in Walnut Grove, MO. All Mike's Bar-BQ meats are smoked with plenty of Ozark Hickory wood also from the Family Farm.

"The Big Rick"
(for the hearty eater)

Brisket or pulled pork
   (smoked with Ozark Hickory wood)
Crisp bacon
Fresh buns

Your favorite BBQ sauce
Sautéed or grilled mushrooms
Swiss cheese

Directions

Pile meat high on a bun with BBQ sauce. Then smother with sautéed mushrooms and bacon bits. Melt Swiss cheese over the top.

Submitted by Mike Whittenberg, owner

1252 Hwy. KK
Osage Beach, MO 65065
(573) 348-1735

Mitch & Duff's at Dogwood Hills is named after two of the owners who have also served as golf pros for Dogwood Hills Golf Club. When the clubhouse was remodeled and expanded to accommodate the restaurant, many names were suggested for the new facility, but it finally came down to this simple and descriptive name.

Hillbilly French Toast

12 large eggs
1 Tbsp. vanilla extract
1 Tbsp. sugar
12 slices Texas toast

¼ c. half and half
1 tsp. ground cinnamon
2 c. Frosted Flakes

Directions

Coarse grind Frosted Flakes and put aside in a flat pan or dish. Combine eggs, half and half, vanilla, cinnamon and sugar in a bowl and whip well. Heat grill to 400° and spray generously with non-stick spray. Dip bread in egg batter and then dip bread in crushed frosted flakes, shake and turn over and repeat on other side. Cook until golden brown, turn over and repeat. Cut diagonally. Serve on large plate and garnish with powdered sugar and orange slice. Add your favorite breakfast meat and you will have a breakfast everyone will rave about!

Submitted by Ron Schlicht, general manager

MYRTLE'S PLACE BACKALLEY BBQ

109 N. Broadway
Poplar Bluff, MO 63901
(573) 785-9203

Myrtle's Place Backalley BBQ is family owned and operated. Debbie and Tommy Sliger have owned the restaurant for 10 years. Myrtle's is located downtown across from the Rodger's theatre. This family owned restaurant offers a variety of services. A few of these services are breakfast anytime, daily lunch specials, BBQ, and homemade pies. They also have meeting rooms, smoking and non-smoking areas, to go orders, and holiday cooking that could meet your special needs.

Business hours are Monday thru Friday 5 a.m. to 3 p.m., Saturday 5 a.m. to 2 p.m., and closed on Sunday. You can contact them at 573-785-9203. Please stop by Myrtle's Place Backalley BBQ were good service, and a smile awaits you.

LaLa's Crock Pot Dressing

2 pkg. cornbread mix
4 eggs
2 cans cream of chicken
Chopped onions

1 16-0z. pkg. chicken stuffing mix
2 cans cream of celery
3 cans chicken broth
Butter

Directions

First, cook package cornbread mix (follow directions on mix), and then cook on a cookie sheet. Let cool, and then put baked cornbread in crock pot.

Add all ingredients into crock pot. Chop onions if desired. Stir everything up, and then put squirt butter on top. Let cook in crock pot for 2 hours on high or 4 hours on low. Stir occasionally, and add little water if to dry.

This recipe is awesome. My family asks me to bring it on every holiday.

Submitted by Debbie Sliger, owner

PEPPERCORNS RESTAURANT & BAKERY

2421 W. Highway 76
Branson, MO 65616
(417) 335-6699

For quality country-cooked goodness in a spacious and charming Victorian setting, Peppercorn's is the place to go for the taste of Home Cookin'. Peppercorn's has full menu service along with their delicious Buffets, Breakfast (7 AM to 11 AM) and Lunch (11 AM to 4 PM). Two Dinner Buffets are offered starting at 4 PM till close, featuring a Country Buffet and the Seafood Buffet (through Sept 15) with Crab-Legs and Boiled Shrimp. Plus much, much more!

"Twice Baked" Garlic Mashed Potatoes

Mashed potatoes
Margarine or butter

Garlic pepper

Directions

Grease a full sheet pan with butter. Spread mashed potatoes evenly on pan about 1" in thickness. Sprinkle with garlic pepper, drizzle butter on top and back at 350° for 10-12 minutes. Slice into squares and serve.

Submitted by Peppercorn's staff

Ruby Lena's Tea Room

224 W. Main
Branson, MO 65616
Phone and fax (417) 239-2919

My husband, Dwain, and I opened our restaurant in 2002. It is in a 100 year old home that I had admired for years. We renovated it and opened in 2002. We named it after our mothers. We have a different menu everyday with a few local favorites every day. One of those is our homemade coconut cream pie that my husband makes "from scratch." Yes ladies, "my husband."

Spinach Quiche with Sun Dried Tomatoes

1 10" pie crust
1 tsp. oregano
5 oz. frozen chopped spinach
1¾ c. half-n-half

5 eggs
¼ c. sun dried tomatoes
2 tsp. flour

Directions

Mix flour, oregano, half-n-half. Add thawed spinach, sun dried tomatoes and beaten eggs. Mix well and add 2 cups shredded Mozzarella cheese. Place in crust and bake at 350° for 45 minutes.

Submitted by Sherrie & Dwain Thompson, owners

SCALLIONS

OTC's student operated upscale restaurant

Located at Ozarks Technical Community College
Info Commons Building, West End
1001 E. Chestnut Expwy. • Springfield, MO 65806
(417) 447-8283

Scallions is the student operated upscale eatery located on the campus of Ozarks Technical Community College in the Information Commons West building. Scallions opened it's doors to the public in 2001 as a method for upper level students to have the opportunity to work in a real world restaurant setting learning all aspects of the restaurant from front to the back. The Scallions menu and logo changes every semester to reflect changing food trends and to allow students to experience a wide range of culture and cuisines. From Greek to Mexican to a taste of Georgia each semester provides a menu that is unique and special. Scallions is open to the general public and walk in are welcome but reservations are definitely recommended.

Shrimp with Tomato and Feta

2 Tbsp. olive oil
1 ea. garlic clove, minced
2 Tbsp. tomato paste
1 tsp. basil
2 Tbsp. black olives, sliced
¾ c. shrimp stock (made double strength)
1½ c. cooked orzo pasta
Salt and pepper to taste

2 Tbsp. onion
½ c. diced tomato with juice
1½ tsp. oregano
7 ea. shrimp, peeled and deveined
¼ c. Feta cheese, crumbled
2 Tbsp. fresh lemon juice
1 tsp. fresh oregano

Directions

In a medium skillet, warm the oil over medium-high heat until hot. Add the onion and garlic and cook until the mixture is golden, about 3 minutes. Add the tomatoes, oregano, basil and pepper, tomato paste, lemon juice and shrimp stock and bring the mixture to a boil over medium heat. Add the shrimp and cook for two minutes. Add in the olives and the COOKED orzo pasta and half the feta cheese, stir to combine. Serve in a large soup bowl. Crumble remaining feta cheese on top with fresh parsley and the fresh oregano.

*Follow the package directions for making the orzo. Toss with salt and pepper and olive oil to hold for service.

Submitted by Chef Lou Rice

SILVER STAR STEAKHOUSE & SALOON

5089 Flat River Rd.
Farmington, MO 63640
(573) 431-0301

The Silver Star Steakhouse & Saloon was founded in 2004 by a local businessman. "Old Highway 67", currently known as Flat River Road, used to be a dotted landscape of small saloons and taverns. The "Silver Star" was a local saloon along with such others as Melody Inn, Redneck Mother and Clover Club.

This area is also known for its history of lead mining which was a way of life for many local residents. Country living is also an important link to the past as well as the present.

Hot Pepper Cheese Potatoes

3 lb. cubed potatoes	½ stick butter
1 tsp. salt	¾ tsp. black pepper
1¼ tsp. garlic powder	1¼ tsp. onion powder
1½ tsp. Lawry's Season salt	8 oz. Pepper Jack cheese, shredded

Directions

Cube potatoes and place in casserole dish. Cover about ½ way with water and melt ½ stick of margarine and drizzle over top.

Season generously with salt, pepper, garlic powder, onion powder and Lawry's Season salt. Bake in oven at 350° until potatoes are tender (about 45 minutes). Uncover and top with shredded Pepper Jack cheese. Mix the cheese through the potatoes and place more shredded cheese on top. Bake until cheese is melted. Serve while hot.

Submitted by Elmer Anderson, manager

SILVER STAR STEAKHOUSE & SALOON

5089 Flat River Rd.
Farmington, MO 63640
(573) 431-0301

The Silver Star Steakhouse & Saloon was founded in 2004 by a local businessman. "Old Highway 67", currently known as Flat River Road, used to be a dotted landscape of small saloons and taverns. The "Silver Star" was a local saloon along with such others as Melody Inn, Redneck Mother and Clover Club.

This area is also known for its history of lead mining which was a way of life for many local residents. Country living is also an important link to the past as well as the present.

Mexican Casserole

4 c. prepared rice (your choice)
1 small onion
1½ lbs. Velveeta cheese
1 can refried beans
1 pkg. taco seasoning

1½ lbs. ground beef
1 c. milk
1 can diced tomatoes
1 can condensed cheese soup
1 c. shredded cheddar cheese

Directions

Prepare rice and place in a casserole dish. Brown ground beef with chopped onion. Drain off excess grease and discard. Add ½ to 1 cup water, diced tomatoes and refried beans. Stir in package of taco seasoning and simmer mixture until combined.

Pour over rice in casserole dish.

Pour milk into sauce pan. Melt in Velveeta cheese and condensed cheese soup. Simmer over medium heat until combined, stirring constantly. When smooth and creamy, pour over rice and meat mixture and top with shredded cheddar cheese. Bake in oven at 350° for about 30 minutes. Serve with tortilla chips for dipping or place over bed of lettuce, jalapenos and tomatoes for an alternative taco salad.

Submitted by Elmer Anderson, manager

Smitty's Smoke Shack

Bar-B-Que

**226-A Highway 125 South
Sparta, MO 65753
(417) 634-2545**

Smitty's Smoke Shack Bar-B-Que is a small family-owned and operated restaurant in Sparta, Missouri. We serve smoked and/or Bar-B-Qued meats, beef brisket, pulled pork and our specialty pork spareribs. We feature our own homemade Bar-B-Que sauce, baked beans and salads. The meats are smoked with a combination of hickory or cherry woods.

Benson's Baked Beans

1 large onion
1 green bell pepper
1 yellow bell pepper
7 lb. 3 oz. can pork 'n beans
1 Tbsp. ceyenne pepper

½ c. garlic, minced
1 red bell pepper
1 lb. bacon
1 lb. brown sugar

Directions

Saute onion, bell peppers and garlic. Fry bacon and all ingredients. Simmer for 30 minutes. Serves 18-20 people.

Submitted by Mike and Linda Benson

ST. MICHAEL'S

301 South Avenue
Springfield, MO
(417) 865-2315

Although the names have changed over the past 32 years, the style remains consistent. Owner/operators Nick and Jenny Russo have a long standing history in the local restaurant industry. St. Michael's, located at the corner of South and McDaniel, in Springfield, MO, has evolved from Pop's Malt Shop, Ebbets Field (both the Cherry Street and Walnut Street locations) and Russo's Café and Market. Their most recent project is an intimate (65-70 seat) sports eatery located in the heart of the downtown revival. Jenny, a former Kansas City resident, operates St. Michael's during the daytime hours and has developed a reputation for her fresh soups and gourmet sandwiches and currently boasts that she can make 3 sandwiches to her husband's one. Three to two may be a more realistic ratio. St. Michael's continues with their tradition of serving fresh 1/2 pound burgers and fresh-cut fries. The restaurant is available for private gatherings while catering is also available.

Shrimp Marinara Sauce

20 oz. can of quality whole peeled tomatoes (Progresso)
2 fresh garlic cloves
3 leaves of large fresh basil

Extra virgin olive oil
1 lb. of large shrimp
Salt and pepper
Grated Picarino Romano cheese

Directions

Cover the bottom of a medium pan with olive oil; add the chopped garlic, cooked over a low flame until tender but not brown. Add fresh basil, salt and pepper. Add a can of whole peeled tomatoes (hand crushed not blended). Cook for 10 minutes, stirring occasionally. Add cleaned, peeled and deveined raw shrimp. Cook for 15 additional minutes. Add this sauce over your favorite pasta and top with grated Romano cheese. Serve with Italian bread and your favorite glass of wine. My father once warned "who's gonna tell me I can't drink Chianti with my calamari?"

Submitted by Nick & Jenny Russo, owners

The BROWN BAG

825 E. Hwy. 60
Monett, MO 65708
(417) 236-0272

This sandwich is a signature sandwich for the Brown Bag, which was founded in Monett, MO in 2004. The Brown Bag was originally started to be a small espresso shop and deli but as since grown to a full service gourmet coffee shop and very busy deli and bakery. The owner is at the moment looking at a larger second location and working on franchising The Brown Bag. Billie, the owner, offers full service catering for any occasion from birthdays to weddings to banquets. She specializes in custom cake decorating to compliment any occasion.

"The HOT STUFF" grilled roast beef

Sauce
½ c. real mayonnaise
½ c. horseradish
1 Tbsp. ground pepper

2 slice whole wheat bread
2 slices Provolone cheese
3 oz. lean roast beef

Directions

Spread the sauce on each slice of bread. Lay on a slice of the Provolone cheese and add the roast beef. Grill on a panini grill for 3 minutes.

Submitted by Billie Walters

102 N. Union Street
Mtn. Grove, MO 65711
(417) 926-7565

The Cajun Kettle is a family owned and run restaurant. We serve high quality food at affordable prices. It is owned and run by Melissa Cantrelle and her husband Everett who were born and raised in Louisiana. This recipe was created for a quick meal. When you don't have a lot of time, mix it and let the oven do the rest.

Meat Loaf Muffins

2 lb. ground chuck
1 small bell pepper
½ tsp. garlic powder or
  1 garlic pod, smashed
½ c. BBQ sauce

1 med. onion
2 stalks of celery
Cajun seasoning
1 egg, medium
BBQ sauce to top

Directions

Mix all ingredients together. Spray your muffin pan and shape your meat mixture into palm size balls and put into pan. top with a little spoon of BBQ Sauce. bake at 400° for 20 minutes. Serve with smashed potatoes.

Submitted by The Cajun Kettle

THE RAILS CATFISH & SEAFOOD BUFFET

433 Animal Safari Rd.
Branson, MO 65616
(417) 336-3401

Known for its Catfish, Seafood & Country Cooking, The Rails has been a local's favorite since 1993. Located off the strip, the stars and visitors alike appreciate the laid back, family atmosphere as well as the southern favorites like homemade gumbo and cinnamon rolls.

Twice Baked Potatoes

10 medium to large baked potatoes
½ stick butter (melted)
1 c. crumbled bacon (cooked)
1 c. shredded cheddar cheese

1 Tbsp. garlic herb seasoning
½ c. onion
1 tsp. pepper
1 tsp. salt

Directions

Leave skin on and cut potato in half. Scoop out most of potato in bowl and put skin boats on greased baking sheet. After removing potatoes, mash well and add other ingredients. Mix well and put back in skin boats. Bake at 375° till browned.

Submitted by Sheri Stevens, manager

UNDERCLIFF GRILL & BAR

6385 Old Highway 71
Joplin, MO 64804
(417) 623-8382
www.undercliff.com

The Undercilff Grill & Bar is nestled into the side of a cliff serving locals and tourists a like. The atmosphere is comfortable and the food is wonderful. You can kick back and enjoy our decor, mostly supplied by the locals. Our guests love to bring in friends and family because they feel that it is a home away from home.

Dry Rub for Pork or Beef

2 c. brown sugar
¾ c. garlic salt
2 oz. cumin
1 oz. cayenne pepper

1 c. onion salt
4 oz. chili seasoning
2 oz. mustard seed

Directions

Rub this on the pork or beef before cooking. After cooking glaze the meat with barbeque sauce for 15 minutes.

Submitted by Mike Winn, owner

VALENTINE'S RESTAURANT

2902-B South Campbell
Springfield, MO, 65807
(417) 891-9700
www.valentinesrestaurant.com

STEAKS • PASTA • SEAFOOD

Casual dining at its finest, in an elegant, sophisticated, yet contemporary casual setting. Menu offers hand cut steaks, pasta, seafood, salads, sandwiches & lunch menu. Sunday brunch, full liquor, beer & wine, outside patio seating, happy hour daily 4 p.m.-7 p.m., late night happy hour 9 p.m.-close. Lunch & Dinner, 7 Days. Reservations welcome.

Strawberry Balsamic Vinaigrette

1½ c. strawberry mix, 4 to 1
½ c. dark brown sugar
¼ tsp. salt
¼ c. salad oil

1 c. Balsamic vinegar
½ c. honey
¼ tsp. nutmeg

Directions

Combine all ingredients in food processor or blender except for the salad dressing, blend on high setting for approx. ten seconds. With the food processor or blender on high, drizzle the salad oil into the processor slowly to emulsify.

Cover, Label, Date, Initial. Do Not Refrigerate. Shelf life: 14 days; Yield: 4 cups.

Submitted by Joseph Sunseri, owner

WAGON WHEEL STEAKHOUSE & FAMILY RESTAURANT

**2130 N. Main
(next to Walmart)
Mtn. Grove, MO
(417) 926-5471**

Wagon Wheel Steakhouse & Family Restaurant is locally owned and operated. In addition to serving delicious buffets we have a large selection of items on our menu to choose from including some of the best steaks in the area. We also have a private dining room for large groups or special occasions. Come in and experience some down-home cooking.

Hush Puppies

3 c. cornmeal
3 tsp. baking powder
1½ tsp. baking soda
1½ tsp. onion salt
2¼ to 3 c. buttermilk

1½ c. flour
3 tsp. salt
¾ tsp. garlic powder
3 eggs, beaten
1 med. onion, chopped fine

Directions

Mix dry. Then wet together. Spoon small amount into a deep fryer at 350°.

Egg Noodles

18 eggs
12 c. flour

2 c. Sprite
6 tsp. salt

Directions

Mix eggs and Sprite together. Then mix with flour and salt. Flour table well, divide into quarters. Take out 1 quarter and knead until easy to handle. Roll out until very thin and cut into strips. Flour and let dry for a few minutes before cooking.

Submitted by Mary Lou Meierotto

ZIGGIE'S CAFE

5 LOCATIONS:

2222 South Campbell Ave.
Springfield, MO – 24 Hours

853 North Glenstone Ave.
Springfield, MO– 24 Hours

1324 West Kearny St.
Springfield, MO – 5 a.m. - 11 p.m.

901 North Kenneth
Nixa, MO – 6 a.m.-10 p.m.

1230 West Hwy. 80
Republic, MO – 6 a.m. - 10 p.m.

All Ziggie's Cafe locations phone number:
(417) 883-0900
www.ziggiescafe.com

Ziggie's Café is a 24 hour family owned and operated restaurant that specializes in friendly service. We have been serving the Springfield area for over 20 years. We take pride in our loyal customers and the service that we provide for them. Our goals are to provide a friendly atmosphere, fast service, and great food, 7 days a week.

Our menu is one of the largest in the city; offering breakfast served anytime, as well as sandwiches, pastas, steaks, and desserts.

We also offer take out dining and provide full catering service. (417) 881-5154

Gift cards are available to purchase and may be used at any location.

Tuscany Benedict

2 pieces Italian Focaccia Bread
⅛ c. chopped onions
⅛ c. sliced black olives
⅛ c. sliced mushrooms
Pinch of parsley

1 Tbsp. olive oil
⅛ c. diced tomatoes
⅛ c. thinly sliced Prosciutto ham
4 large eggs

Directions

Slice and place Focaccia bread open on plates. Saute vegetables and ham in pan with olive oil until cooked but still firm. Top Focaccia bread with vegetable and ham. Pour creamy pesto sauce all over mix. Top with 2 eggs cooked your way. Sprinkle parsley over top of food.

Pesto Sauce:
1 c. fresh basil
½ c shredded asiago cheese
  (non-processed Parmesan is fine, too)
¼ c, extra virgin olive oil

4 cloves garlic
1 tsp. coarse black pepper
Salt to taste

Process the first six ingredients in a food processor until uniformly chopped. Gradually add the olive oil while the processor is running. You'll definitely want to taste and add things as needed. Consistency will be a fairly thick paste.

Submitted by Ziggie's staff

★★★★★ R E S T A U R A N T

Recipes of

DESSERTS

A SLICE OF PIE

601 Kingshighway
Rolla, MO
(573) 364-6203

The pies are glorious at A Slice of Pie: the velvet-cream meringues, the Boston cream, and the Tahitian cream are especially noteworthy, that last one being a layered pie of sliced bananas, pudding, and pineapple with a mantle of toasted coconut on top. A little eatery halfway between St. Louis and Springfield, there are far too many pies (not to mention cakes and cheesecakes!) for even the biggest appetites to try some of everything in just a few visits.

The problem of eating one's way through the dessert menu is compounded by the fact that lunch and supper at A Slice of Pie are hearty. After a bowl of wonderful home-made creamy tomato soup or potato soup with bacon, try a flake-crusted chicken mushroom pot pie. Make sure to save room for dessert on each visit!

Coconut Buttermilk Custard

4 eggs
1 Tbsp. flour
¼ c. half & half
1 tsp. lemon juice

1½ c. sugar
1½ c. buttermilk
1 stick butter, melted
⅔ c. coconut

Directions

Combine. Pour into one unbaked pie shell. Bake at 350° for 50 minutes to an hour.

Submitted by Ron and Mickey Hopson

1622 Horseshoe Bend Pkwy.
P.O. Box 1547
Lake Ozark, MO 65049
(573) 365-2800

Andre's Restaurant - an inviting restaurant situated atop a bluff overlooking The Lake of the Ozarks, provides diners a change from the Ordinary. It is located on Horseshoebend Parkway, close to resorts and hotels The owner Andre Torres, a certified executive chef, oversees the daily operation. Andre's food transports diners around a world of culinary delights-steaks grilled on a woodfire grill, lobster with a champagne butter, chicken, fish, veal, and pasta. Inside Andre's, make sure you have a martini at Le Fou Bar - (a great bar with a vast martini list, specialty drinks, and a light bar menu) During summer do not miss Sunday Brunch from 9:00AM-1:00PM. Cooking classes September to May at 6:00 PM International night every third Friday of the Month.

Gateau Basque

1 c. + 3 oz. flour, sifted
7 oz. butter, unsalted
⅓ c. almond flour
Peel of 1 lemon, grated
Pinch of salt

7 oz. sugar
2 large egg yolks
1 whole large egg
1 Tbsp. almond extract or rum

Filling:

1 c. cherry/brandy preserves   3 c. almond flavored pastry cream
(All these items available at gourmet shops. If your pastry cream recipe is sweet, take most of the sugar out of it)

Directions

Cream the sugar and butter. Add the eggs one at a time. Add almond flour, zest and vanilla. Add flour all at one time and just mix. Chill for 1 hour, this dough is very soft.

Cut the dough into 2 pieces (1 10 oz. and the other 22 oz.) Roll the 22 oz. dough to about ¼" thick and line at 10" x 1¾-2" deep tart pan.

Put ⅔ of the cherry preserves into the tart pan and cover the bottom. Put enough pastry cream in the tart to allow for the remaining preserves and the top crust.

Top the pastry cream with the remaining preserves and rollout the 10 oz. crust. Crimp the top and bottom crusts together. Top with 10 oz. crust and egg wash and scrape designs in the top with a fork.

Bake at 400° for 10 minutes, turn oven down to 325° for 20-25 minutes. A lower rack is better to get the bottom crust done.

Submitted Andre Torres, owner and executive chef

BLACK KETTLE

10 E. Broadway
Monett, MO 65708
(417) 235-7199

The Black Kettle has been serving Monett and Southwest Missouri residents for more than 50 years. Famous for its Black Kettle Salads, the menu includes prime rib, charbroiled steaks, BBQ, seafood, burgers and sandwiches. The Black Kettle also has the best breakfast in town.

Coconut Cream Pie

1. 1 c. sugar
2. ½ c. cornstarch
3. 5 egg yolks
4. ½ tsp. salt
5. 1 tsp. vanilla
6. 3 c. milk
7. 2 Tbsp. butter
8. 1 c. snowflake coconut
9. 5 egg whites
10. ½ tsp. salt
11. 1 tsp. vanilla
12. ½ c. sugar
13. 3 tsp. cornstarch

Directions

Filling: Stir the fist 8 ingredients together. Boil until thick, put into a cooked pie shell to cool.

Beat ingredients 9 thru 11 until stiff. Add ingredients 12 and 13 mixed together, beat again until stiff. Put top on filling, sprinkle with coconut snowflakes. Bake for 15 minutes at 350°.

Submitted by Cindy Plemons, chef

Boardwalk Grill

401 N. Main
Laurie, MO 65038
(573) 374-6002

The Boardwalk Grill is a relaxed and casual seafood and steak house located in Laurie, Missouri. Steve and Nick Stock (owner/general manager) constructed the Boardwalk Grill in the spring of 2004. Operations began in early August of 2004. Open All Year at 11:00 a.m., Monday - Saturday. We hope that you enjoy a few of our favorite dishes!

Country Apple Dessert

1 box Pillsbury Plus yellow cake mix
1 egg
½ c. brown sugar, packed
1 tsp. cinnamon
1 egg

⅓ c. butter, softened
1 (20 oz.) can apple pie filling
½ c. walnuts, chopped
1 c. sour cream
1 tsp. vanilla

Directions

Preheat oven to 350°. In a large bowl, combine cake mix, butter and egg, at low speed with electric mixer to form a crumbly dough. Press mixture into bottom of an ungreased 9 x 13 inch pan. Spread apple pie filling over top. Combine brown sugar, nuts and cinnamon. Sprinkle over pie filling. Combine sour cream, egg and vanilla, pour over top. Bake 40 to 55 minutes or until golden brown.

Submitted by Nicholas Stock, general manager

**Located in Historic Downtown A block
from the Mississippi Riverfront
120 North Main Street
Cape Girardeau, Missouri 63701
(573) 334-7235
www.broussardscajuncuisine.com**

On June 10, 1987, Barron and Kathy Broussard opened up Broussard's Cajun Cuisine with a handful of family recipes, determined to bring a taste of the bayous of Southwest Louisiana to the Midwest. Broussard's offers scrumptious Cajun food like etouffee, shrimp creole, crawfish, and alligator specialties, as well as delicious classics such as steak, ribs, burgers, and po' boys. Broussard's takes pride in its laid back Beale Street atmosphere, with live entertainment every Friday & Saturday, and a staff with plenty of personality! In February 2004, Hunter and Stephanie Clark bought Broussard's and have continued the traditions that Barron and Kathy sought to achieve, while always striving to dazzle their guests with excellent service and a very unique dining experience. You can visit them on the web at www.broussardscajuncuisine.com

Broussard's Bread Pudding with Rum Sauce

½ lb. butter
3 c. sugar
5 eggs
2 loaves white sandwich bread

3 cans (12 oz.) milnot
¼ gal. of 2% milk
1½ Tbsp. cinnamon

Directions

Fill two 9½ x 12 cake pans with white bread torn up, set aside. Mix butter, milnot, sugar and milk in stockpot on medium heat until almost boiling. Mix eggs together and then add to mixture. Add only 1 Tbsp. cinnamon mixture. Pour mixture on top of torn bread. Sprinkle ½ Tbsp. of cinnamon on top. Cook at 325° for about 45 minutes (check every 20 minutes). Bread pudding should not stick to toothpick when done.

Rum Sauce:
½ lb. butter
3 c. sugar
¼ gal. of 2% milk

3 cans (12 oz.) milnot
3 oz. rum

Cook all ingredients on medium heat until almost boiling, stirring constantly. Pour onto bread pudding. Makes about 20 pieces with a ½ gal. of rum sauce.

Submitted by Stephanie Clark

37 Court Square
West Plains, MO 65775
(417) 256-3780
www.cafe37.biz

Café 37 is located in the historic Opera House in West Plains, MO, featuring steaks, seafood, and specialty fare served in an elegant yet comfortable atmosphere. Soon after owners Toni and Dennis Johnson opened Café 37 on the historic downtown Square it quickly earned a reputation as the area's premiere dining establishment. From the original hardwood floors to the ornate tin ceilings, the turn-of-the-century ambience sets the stage for fabulous food, superior service, and an extensive selection of wines, beers and top-shelf liquors. For special occasions or a night out with family or friends visit Café 37 for a memorable dining experience.

Toll House Pie

2 eggs
½ c. brown sugar
6 oz. chocolate chips
1, 9-in. pie crust (in pan)

½ c. flour
1 c. butter, melted and cooled
1 c. chopped pecans (or other nut)

Directions

Preheat oven to 325°. Beat eggs until foamy. Add flour and sugars. Beat. Blend in melted butter. Stir in chips and nuts. Pour into unbaked pie shell. Bake at 325° for 1 hour. Let set until cool.

Submitted by Toni Chritton-Johnson, owner

CAFE GLAIZE

Inn at Grand Glaize
Hwy. 54, Lake Road 40
Osage Beach, MO 65065
(573) 348-4731

At Café Glaize, our Executive Chef David Harkins and his culinary team take pride in the quality and presentation of each meal. Choose from an array of tempting dishes, we have a wide range of options available – from formal "Gold Medal Dining" to our casual Ozark Barbecue or go casual with finger foods. Banquet services, breakfast meetings, boardroom lunches, carefree themed parties and elaborate ballroom dining can all be catered to suit your needs.

Chocolate Nut Ricotta Cheesecake

12 oz. chocolate cookie crumbs
Non stick pan spray
3 Tbsp. butter
2 lbs. ricotta cheese
10 oz. sugar
8 oz. whole eggs

4 oz. unsweetened cocoa powder
3 tsp. all-purpose flour
1 tsp. vanilla extract
8 oz. sour cream
6 oz. chopped nuts

Directions

Preheat oven to 350°, grease 2 9-inch springform pans. Combine cookie crumbs and butter, mix well. Press evenly over bottom and up an inch or so in the pans. Chill. Beat ricotta cheese with a hand mixer with a paddle attachment. Slowly blend in the sugar and eggs. On a low setting, add cocoa, flour and vanilla until well blended. Add sour cream and blend on a low setting. Mix in nuts. Pour half of mixture into each pan. Bake about 1 hour or until cakes set. Chill cakes overnight. Remove from pans and serve. Each cake serves 12 to 14 slices.

Submitted by David E. Harkins, executive chef

CLARION HOTEL SPRINGFIELD

Banquets & Catering

3333 S. Glenstone
Springfield, MO 65804
(417) 883-6550
www.clarionhotel-spfld.com

BY CHOICE HOTELS

The Clarion Hotel & Conference Center features 193 guestrooms including Suites & a Jacuzzi Suite. It offers over 17,000 sq. feet of meeting space. The conference center can accommodate groups from 10 to 700 guests. It's the perfect location for Corporate Meetings, Weddings, Reunions and Social Events. Being locally owned and operated, the Clarion has established a reputation of providing excellent guest service, excellent accommodations and delicious food.

Mocha Cappuccino Whip

½ pt. heavy whipping cream
½ c. chocolate syrup
½ tsp. vanilla

½ c. powdered sugar
1 Tbsp. instant coffee

Directions

Combine all ingredients in a chilled bowl. Whip with electric mixer on high until stiff peak forms. Serve over fudge brownie, cheesecake, your favorite dessert or coffee drink.

Submitted by Chef John Blansit

COOKIN' FROM SCRATCH

I-44 Exit 179
Doolittle, MO
(573) 762-3111

Located midway between St. Louis and Springfield, MO. Cookin' from Scratch is a favorite stop for the traveler and most importantly, our local clientele. Whether your favorite meal is breakfast, lunch or dinner, we have a unique variety of offering to satisfy the most demanding palette. Our huge iron skillets fry up some of the most delicious chicken anywhere around. It's so good no one has ever tried to copy it, as so many other restaurants try to steal someone else's good idea.

Fruit Short Cake

Variety muffin mix (or your favorite short cake recipe)

Fresh fruit filling (canned pie filling)
Whipped cream (whipped on top)

Directions

Cook short cake mixture according to package directions. (So that it is about 2 inches high when finished baking.) When cool cut into 4x4 squares. Slice square in half so that you have a top and a bottom. Add filling to top of bottom square. Put top on. Decorate with whipped cream.

Variations could include fresh strawberries, your favorite "wet" fruit or use strawberries, pineapple, bananas, cherries and chocolate sauce to make a banana split.

Submitted by Tony Sherrer, owner

"Where we treat you like family."

Hwy. 5
Laurie, MO 65038
(573) 374-0922

Cousins is a family restaurant known for its homestyle country cooking. The servers are a little sassy, but the customers wouldn't have it any other way.

Crunchy Caramel Apple Pie

1 single pie crust
3 Tbsp. sugar
⅛ tsp. salt
Crumb Topping Mix
  1 c. brown sugar
  ½ c. quick cooking oats
  ½ c. pecans

½ c. sugar plus
1 tsp. cinnamon
6 c. cooking apples, sliced thin

½ c. flour
½ c. butter
¼ c. caramel ice cream topping

Directions

Mix first ingredients and add apples. Toss. Use pastry blender for crumb topping ingredients and stir. Put apple mixture in crust. Sprinkle crumb topping. Bake at 375° for 25 minutes with foil over edge of pie crust. Remove foil. Bake 25-30 minutes more. Remove from oven. Sprinkle ½ c. chopped pecans and drizzle ¼ c. caramel ice cream topping over pie. Cool.

Submitted by Valerie Ites, partner

I'M HOOKED ON DOWD'S CATFISH AND B·B·Q

LEBANON, MO

1760 W. Elm
Lebanon, MO 65536
(417) 532-1777

This is one of our customer's favorite desserts. Rich, tasty, but not too filling. We also have a large variety of cakes, cheesecakes, cookies and pies. Come on in and let us know which is your favorite.

Brownie Delight

2-in. square cooked brownie
 (see recipe page 169)
Chocolate syrup

2 scoops rich vanilla ice cream
Whipped cream

Directions

Heat the brownie in a microwave for one minute on a 10" round plate. Put the 2 scoops of ice cream on the corners (across from each other) of the brownie. Put 4 dollops of whipped cream around the plate and one final one in the center of the brownie. Drizzle the top with chocolate syrup. This is a quick and easy dessert and yet looks very impressive when served.

Submitted by Gary Dyer, owner

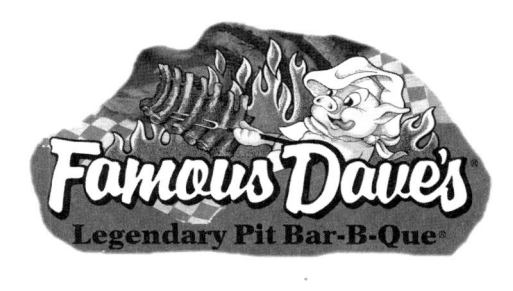

**New Location
At Branson Landing
Branson, MO
COMING SOON**

The recipe is part of a collection of "Down Home" cooking in Dave's fabulous book Famous Dave's Backroads and Sidestreets (proceeds from the book benefit charity). If the fruit should stick to the skillet, Dave says not to worry, just remove it and place it back on top of the cake.

Famous Dave's Pineapple Upside-Down Cake

⅔ c. packed light brown sugar
2 tsp. vanilla extract, divided
9 canned pineapple slices
2 egg yolks
½ c. sugar
2 tsp. baking powder
¼ c. shortening
¼ c. half and half

⅓ + ¼ c. butter, softened, divided
½ tsp. cinnamon
9 maraschino cherry halves
2 egg whites, stiffly beaten
1½ c. flour
¾ tsp. salt
¼ c. pineapple juice
¼ c. buttermilk

Directions

Preheat oven to 350° F. Mix brown sugar and ⅓ c. butter in a bowl. Stir in 1 tsp. vanilla and cinnamon. Spread evenly over the bottom of an ungreased 9" cast iron skillet or a 9" x 9" baking pan. Heat until the brown sugar melts.

Arrange pineapple slices over the brown sugar mixture. Place a cherry half in the middle of each slice. Beat egg yolks in a mixer bowl until thickened. Gradually add ½ c. sugar, beating constantly until blended.

Mix flour, baking powder and salt together in a large mixing bowl. Add shortening, ¼ c. butter, pineapple juice, half and half, buttermilk and 1 tsp. vanilla. Beat until blended, scraping the bowl occasionally. Mix in egg yolk mixture. Fold in stiffly beaten egg whites.

Spoon the batter into the prepared skillet. Bake for 35 - 40 minutes or until a cake tester comes out clean. Invert the skillet onto a serving platter, allowing the skillet to rest on the cake for several minutes before removing.

Submitted by Famous Dave

KALDI'S COFFEE HOUSE

900 Battlefield Rd. #139
Springfield, MO 65807
(417) 881-5546

KALDI'S
Coffee Roasting Company

The original Kaldi's Coffeehouse is situated in the historical DeMun neighborhood of Clayton overlooking Concordia Park. We first opened our doors here in 1994. In 2005 we opened three new coffeehouses, two in St. Louis and one in Springfield, Missouri.

Oatmeal Nut Trail Bars

1⅔ c. shelled nuts or nuts and seeds (any combination, such as ⅓ c. each of pecans, walnuts, pistachios and almonds, plus ⅓ c. sunflower kernels)

1 c. (2 sticks) butter, softened
⅔ c. granulated sugar
1 tsp. vanilla
1 tsp. baking soda
3 c. rolled oats
11 c. Kaldi's Caramel Sauced, warmed
   slightly (see recipe below)
¼ c. water
1 c. heavy (40 percent) cream

¾ c. plus 1 tsp. packed light-brown sugar
2 eggs
1½ c. all-purpose flour
1 tsp. ground cinnamon
⅓ c. cracked wheat (such as Hodgson
   Mill Cracked Wheat Hot Cereal_
1½ c. turbinado sugar (see note)
1 tsp. fresh lemon juice
2 Tbsp. butter

Directions

Stir sugar, water and lemon juice together in a heavy medium saucepan; cook and stir over low heat until sugar dissolves, about 12 minutes. Increase the heat, and boil without stirring until the syrup is a deep amber color, about 4 minutes (be careful not to burn). Remove from heat; add cream (the mixture will bubble vigorously). If necessary, stir until any bits of caramel are dissolved. Add butter and whisk until melted. Let cool.

Note: Turbinado sugar is available at some organic food stores and specialty shops. Raw sugar (a light brown, large-crystal sugar available at most supermarkets) may be substituted; it has slightly less molasses flavor.

Preheat the oven to 350°. If the nuts or seeds are very salty, rub them gently in a dry towel to remove some of the salt. Mix together and spread on a cookie sheet; toast until fragrant and beginning to brown, 10 to 12 minutes. Set aside.

Recipe continued on next page

Oatmeal Nut Trailer Bars...continued

Reduce the oven temperature to 300°. Line the bottom and sides of a 9-by-13-inch pan with parchment paper.

In a large mixer bowl, beat butter and sugars until light. Add eggs and vanilla; beat well. Stir together flour, baking soda and cinnamon; add to sugar mixture, beating well. Beat in oats and cracked wheat. Press the dough into the pan; bake until set on top, about 25 minutes.

Carefully spread Kaldi's Caramel Sauce over the baked dough. Firmly press the nut mixture into the caramel. Bake 10 minutes more. Let cool; cut into bars.

Kaldi's Caramel Sauce

1½ c. turbinado sugar (see note)
1 tsp. fresh lemon juice
2 Tbsp. butter

¼ c. water
1 c. heavy (40 percent) cream

Stir sugar, water and lemon juice together in a heavy medium saucepan; cook and stir over low heat until sugar dissolves, about 12 minutes. Increase the heat, and boil without stirring until the syrup is a deep amber color, about 4 minutes (be careful not to burn). Remove from heat; add cream (the mixture will bubble vigorously). If necessary, stir until any bits of caramel are dissolved. Add butter and whisk until melted. Let cool.

Note: Turbinado sugar is available at some organic food stores and specialty shops. Raw sugar (a light brown, large-crystal sugar available at most supermarkets) may be substituted; it has slightly less molasses flavor.

Submitted by Suzanne Langlois, owner

JIMMIE'S
Walleye & Catfish
West Plains, MO
417-256-1538

ALL YOU CAN EAT WALLEYE, CATFISH & SHRIMP

805 Porter Wagoner Blvd.
West Plains, MO 65775
(417) 256-1538

We specialize in fish, fresh cut steaks and BBQ baby back ribs and have been voted Best Breakfast in town. My husband and I met here 7 years ago. I was a waitress. When the restaurant came up for sale we bought it. Now we are here where we met.

Banana Split Cake
This is a great dessert.

1 stick oleo or butter, melted
1 lb. of powdered sugar
2 sticks softened oleo or butter
1 small jar cherries
1 large can crushed pineapple

2 c. crushed Graham crackers
2 eggs
#2 size Cool Whip
4 or 5 bananas
1 pkg. chopped nuts

Directions

Crust: mix together the melted butter and Graham crackers. Put in 9x13 cake pan and set aside. Mix together all other ingredients for no less than 15 minutes. Pour over crust. Add sliced bananas, pineapple and a the Cool Whip. Top with cherries and nuts.

Submitted by Rhonda Powell, kitchen manager

Ozarks Coca-Cola / Dr Pepper Bottling Company

201 Hwy. 72 West
Rolla, MO 65401
(573) 364-4838

Johnny's Smoke Stak has been in business since 1980 serving Burnt Ends and Ribs for the BBQ lovers. We, Lenise & Steven Dowdy, recently purchased Johnny's Smoke Stak on 02-16-06. Since then our goal has been to provide a dining experience that appeals to everyone. Our new expanded menu provides delicious tastes at a reasonable price. Of course, we still serve our famous BBQ Ribs, Burnt Ends, Brisket, Ham, Sausage, Pork, Chicken, and Turkey. Come by for a great meal and remember, we serve bottled beer, wine and many mixed drinks.

This recipe has been in enjoyed by the Harris family for many years. Gladys Harris not only was an extraordinary woman but an excellent cook. She could make a meal out of thin air and make it the most delicious meal that you have ever had the opportunity to taste.

Gladys's Strawberry Cake & Icing

1 white cake mix
½ c. strawberry juice
2 Tbsp. flour
1 c. vegetable oil
Strawberry Cake Icing:
1 lb. box of powdered sugar
2 Tbsp. butter, softened

1 box strawberry Jello
4 whole eggs
½ c. water

1 c. strawberries with juice drained,
  sliced or halved

Directions

Mix all cake ingredients together and bake for approximately one hour at 300 degrees. Take a toothpick and place holes in the cake for the icing to soak in to after removing from the oven.

Icing: Mix all ingredients and drizzle over cake while it is still hot.

Submitted by Johnny's Smoke Stak in memory of Gladys Harris

McFARLAIN'S FAMILY RESTAURANT

AT IMAX® ENTERTAINMENT COMPLEX

Inside the IMAX Complex
3562 Shepherd of the Hills Expressway
Branson, MO 65616
(417) 336-4680

The Ozarks are famous for two things – music and food. The spectacular IMAX Film Ozarks Legacy & Legend documents the musical history of the Ozarks by following the McFarlain family over six generations. Here at McFarlain's, we bring to you the culinary history of the Ozarks with traditional Ozark cooking and recipes that have been handed down from generation to generation. A special place where you can sit back, enjoy your meal and our warm hospitality...for breakfast, lunch and dinner!

Strawberry Rhubarb Pie

2 lbs. frozen or fresh rhubarb
1 c. sugar
¾ c. water
½ c. water

1 small pkg. frozen strawberries
1 Tbsp. salt
1 Tbsp. lemon juice

Directions

Cover rhubarb with water and bring to a boil. Don't overcook. Drain well and let cool. Add sugar, salt and strawberries.

In another bowl mix ¾ c. corn starch, ½ c. water and 1 Tbsp. lemon juice. Stir into fruit-sugar mixture. Cook for 3 minutes, stirring constantly. Pour into pie shell, top with pie dough, brush top of pie with egg wash and sprinkle with sugar, pierce top of pie a few times with a knife to vent. Bake at 350° for 55 minutes or until crust is golden brown.

Submitted by Debby Black, general manager

109 N. Broadway
Poplar Bluff, MO 63901
(573) 785-9203

Myrtle's Place Backalley BBQ is family owned and operated. Debbie and Tommy Sliger have owned the restaurant for 10 years. Myrtle's is located downtown across from the Rodger's theatre. This family owned restaurant offers a variety of services. A few of these services are breakfast anytime, daily lunch specials, BBQ, and homemade pies. They also have meeting rooms, smoking and non-smoking areas, to go orders, and holiday cooking that could meet your special needs.

Business hours are Monday thru Friday 5 a.m. to 3 p.m., Saturday 5 a.m. to 2 p.m., and closed on Sunday. You can contact them at 573-785-9203. Please stop by Myrtle's Place Backalley BBQ were good service, and a smile awaits you.

Grandma Stephen's Carrot Cake

2 c. sugar
2 c. flour
4 eggs
½ tsp. salt
2 tsp. baking soda
1 tsp. vanilla

1½ c. oil
3 c. grated carrots
2 tsp. cinnamon
1 tsp. baking powder
1 c. walnuts

Directions

Mix dry ingredients. Cream oil, eggs, vanilla and sugar. Add 2 mixtures all together and blend well. Bake in an 8x8x2 or 9x13 pan at 350° for 30 minutes or until done.

Frost:

1 box powdered sugar
1 stick butter
1 c. pecan

1 8-oz. cream cheese
1 tsp. vanilla

Cream cheese and butter, then add sugar, vanilla and pecans. Blend well, and add milk if necessary to spread.

Submitted by Debbie Sliger, owner

OTC's student operated upscale restaurant

Located at Ozarks Technical Community College
Info Commons Building, West End
1001 E. Chestnut Expwy. • Springfield, MO 65806
(417) 447-8283

Scallions is the student operated upscale eatery located on the campus of Ozarks Technical Community College in the Information Commons West building. Scallions opened it's doors to the public in 2001 as a method for upper level students to have the opportunity to work in a real world restaurant setting learning all aspects of the restaurant from front to the back. The Scallions menu and logo changes every semester to reflect changing food trends and to allow students to experience a wide range of culture and cuisines. From Greek to Mexican to a taste of Georgia each semester provides a menu that is unique and special. Scallions is open to the general public and walk in are welcome but reservations are definitely recommended.

Pecan Pound Cake with Sautéed Bananas

1½ c. butter
5 eggs
1 tsp. vanilla
4 bananas
4 Tbsp. brown sugar

2 c. all-purpose flour
2 c. white sugar
1½ c. chopped pecans
4 Tbsp. butter
Pinch of salt

Directions

Cream together butter and sugar. Add eggs one at a time beating after each one. Now take 1 cup of the pecans and put in food processor mince. Leave the other ½ cup of pecans just chopped. Blend the flour, vanilla extract, and both pecans minced and chopped. Pour into greased and floured round pan. Bake in a preheated 325° oven for 1 to 1½ hour or until a toothpick inserted comes out with nothing on it. Remove from oven and remove from pan let cool on rake.

Cut quarter piece of cake. Saute bananas in butter and brown sugar. Put bananas on plate then put cake upright in the middle. Drizzle caramel sauce around the cake and top with fresh whipped cream.

Submitted by Chef Lou Rice

SILVER STAR STEAKHOUSE & SALOON

5089 Flat River Rd.
Farmington, MO 63640
(573) 431-0301

The Silver Star Steakhouse & Saloon was founded in 2004 by a local businessman. "Old Highway 67", currently known as Flat River Road, used to be a dotted landscape of small saloons and taverns. The "Silver Star" was a local saloon along with such others as Melody Inn, Redneck Mother and Clover Club.

This area is also known for its history of lead mining which was a way of life for many local residents. Country living is also an important link to the past as well as the present.

Peanut Butter Mini Mud Pies

6 Tbsp. creamy peanut butter
3½ c. coffee ice cream
1 Tbsp. Graham cracker crumbs

6 mini Graham cracker crusts
1 bottle (7 oz.) milk chocolate shell topping

Directions

Spread 1 Tbsp. peanut butter into bottom of each mini crust. Using ½-up or 4 oz. ice cream scoop, place ball of ice cream on each crust. Cover with plastic wrap and freeze for at least 1 hour or until ice cream and crusts are frozen solid.

Remove pies from foil pie tins and place pies on plates. Drizzle chocolate shell topping over ice cream and crusts. Immediately sprinkle ½ tsp. of crumbs over each pie and serve.

Variation: Replace peanut butter with strawberry jam in bottoms of Graham cracker crusts. Replace coffee ice cream with vanilla ice cream. Replace shell topping with strawberry jam,. Add whipped cream and garnish with a fresh cut strawberry.

Submitted by Elmer Anderson, manager

540 Sidney St.
St. James, MO 65559
(800) 280-9463
www.StJamesWinery.com

St. James Winery is owned and operated by the Hofherr Family since 1970, conveniently located on Interstate 44, on Old Historic Route 66 only ninety miles southwest of St. Louis, Missouri in St. James, Missouri .

With over 700 miles of vines in Missouri, Arkansas, and Michigan, no other winery in the Eastern United states utilizes such state of the art technology from the vineyards to the bottling room bringing you consistent quality vintages for your enjoyment. With over 1,800 medals to date, no wonder St. James Winery is "America's Midwest Winery". In our area, be sure to stop by our tasting room and sample our wide variety of vintages, our extensive gift shop, and take a tour of our cellars. St. James Winery products are presently distributed in six states and available on our website.

St. James Winery Blackberry Wine Cake

Cake Ingredients:

1 c. St. James Winery Blackberry Wine
1 box white cake mix
½ c. vegetable oil

½ c. chopped pecans
1 3-oz box berry flavored gelatin
4 eggs

Glaze Ingredients:

1 c. St. James Winery Blackberry Wine
1 stick butter

1 c. powdered sugar

Directions

Preheat over to 350°. Grease and flour a bundt pan. Sprinkle pecans in the bottom. In a large bowl, stir together cake mix and gelatin. Add eggs, oil, and 1 c. of wine. Blend thoroughly. Pour the batter into the prepared pan.

Bake 50-60 minutes until cake tests done. Remove from oven and turn out onto wire rack to cool.

Combine the powdered sugar, butter, and ½ c. wine in a saucepan, bring to a boil. Remove from heat. Pour ½ the mixture over the warm cake. Let set for 30 minutes, then pour remaining glaze, which will have thickened, over the cake.

Order a bottle of St. James Blackberry Wine, and try this delicious recipe!

Submitted by Jack Bonar

SWEET SUSIE'S SWEETS

319½ E. Walnut
Springfield, MO 65806
(417) 880-9659

Sweet Susie's Sweets is quickly becoming a downtown hotspot! Sweet Susie's offers 187 different types of award-winning cheesecakes, many of which are served at restaurants all over town. Try the Gooey Butter Cake or a slice of Red Velvet Cake. For bigger events, ask about full-service catering.

Blonde Brownies

2⅔ c. flour
2½ tsp. baking powder
2¼ c. brown sugar
1 tsp. vanilla
1 c. chopped nuts

½ tsp. salt
⅔ c. butter
3 eggs
12 oz. chocolate chips

Directions

Sift together flour, baking powder and salt. Melt butter, add brown sugar and let cool for 10 minutes. Beat in eggs one at a time. Add flour mixture, vanilla, chips and nuts. Spread in greased 15x10x1 inch pan. Bake at 350° for 25-30 minutes.

Knock Your Socks Off Brownies

1 German chocolate cake mix
¾ c. oleo, softened
1 c. chocolate chips

⅔ c. milnot
1 c. nuts
1 pkg. caramels

Directions

Mix cake mix, ⅓ c. milnot, oleo and nuts together. Press half of mixture in the bottom of a 9x13 inch baking pan and bake for 10 minutes at 350°.

Melt caramels and ⅓ c. milnot together. Sprinkle chocolate chips over hot first layer, then pour caramel mix over that and top with remainder of cake mixture. Bake at 350° for 35 minutes. Cool on a wire rack.

Submitted by Susie & Gerald Wolfe

THE RAILS CATFISH & SEAFOOD BUFFET

433 Animal Safari Rd.
Branson, MO 65616
(417) 336-3401

Known for its Catfish, Seafood & Country Cooking, The Rails has been a local's favorite since 1993. Located off the strip, the stars and visitors alike appreciate the laid back, family atmosphere as well as the southern favorites like homemade gumbo and cinnamon rolls.

Reeses Peanut Butter Cheese Cake

1 8-oz. package cream cheese
1 package Dream Whip
⅓ c. sugar

½ c. milk
1 tsp. vanilla
¼ c. peanut butter

Directions

Mix above ingredients until smooth. Spoon into 8-inch prepared Graham Cracker Crust and top with crumbled Reeses Peanut Butter cups. Freeze or chill before serving.

This is a family favorite and a real crowd pleaser. Enjoy!

Submitted by Sheri Stevens, manager

THE TOWER CLUB

The Tower Club

Twenty-First and Twenty-Second Floors
Atop The Hammons Tower
901 Saint Louis Street
Springfield, MO 65805
(417) 866-4466

The Tower Club is an exclusive town club located in the heart of activity in downtown Springfield. Private parties, luncheons, dinner receptions and meetings for up to 400 people can be accommodated in five private suites, the Starlight Room, or the Main Dining Room. The Tower Club offers panoramic views of the city, superior cuisine, excellent service and the most exquisite dining venue in the city.

Raspberry Cheesecake

Crust:

1½ c. Graham Cracker crumbs
3 oz. butter, melted

1½ Tbsp. sugar

Directions

Mix Graham cracker crumbs, sugar and melted butter together. Press into 10" cake pan. Bake at 350° for 8-10 minutes.

Filling:

1½ lbs. cream cheese
1 Tbsp. vanilla
5 eggs

1 c. sugar
1 c. raspberries

Directions

Mix cream cheese, sugar, vanilla and raspberries together for 5 minutes. Then add eggs and mix for an additional 2 minutes. Pour in to crust and bake for 40-45 minutes at 350° or until firm in center.

Submitted by Vic Pace, pastry chef

WAGON WHEEL STEAKHOUSE & FAMILY RESTAURANT

2130 N. Main
(next to Walmart)
Mtn. Grove, MO
(417) 926-5471

Wagon Wheel Steakhouse & Family Restaurant is locally owned and operated. In addition to serving delicious buffets we have a large selection of items on our menu to choose from including some of the best steaks in the area. We also have a private dining room for large groups or special occasions. Come in and experience some down-home cooking.

Wagon Train Sheet Cake

2 c. flour
1 tsp. baking soda
2 eggs, lightly beaten
½ c. sour cream or ½ c. buttermilk
4 Tbsp. cocoa

2 c. sugar
½ tsp. salt
1 tsp. vanilla
2 sticks butter
1 c. water

Directions

Place 2 sticks of butter, 4 Tbsp. cocoa and 1 c. water over medium heat and bring to a boil. Pour over the flour, sugar and mix well. Add all the other ingredients and mix well. Pour into a well-greased and floured cookie sheet pan (15½x10½). Cookie sheet pan must be a deep cookie sheet pan. Bake at 350° for 23 minutes. Ice cake while it is still hot. Make frosting five minutes before cake is finished.

Chocolate Frosting:

1 stick butter
6 Tbsp. milk
1 c. pecans, chopped

4 Tbsp. cocoa
1 lb. box powdered sugar
½ tsp. vanilla

Mix together butter, cocoa and milk. Cook over medium heat and bring to a boil. Remove from stove and add sugar, nuts and vanilla. Mix well and pour over cake.

Submitted by Mary Lou Meierotto

RESTAURANT

Recipes of

BEVERAGES

AGRARIO RESTAURANT

311 S. Patton
Springfield, MO 65806
(417) 865-4255
www.agrariorestaurant.com

Agrario is an upscale contemporary restaurant in the heart of Downtown Springfield, Mo. Housed in a restored livery stable built in 1860, we stayed true to the original architecture while creating a comfortable modern restaurant. We have two major influences when it comes to food. First we use as much local product as possible. This allows us to be sure that our ingredients are as fresh and flavorful as possible. We combine these local ingredients with influences from the entire Mediterranean region (Spain all the way to North Africa) to create contemporary dishes that represent various seasons. For this reason we change our menus seasonally to best represent the products that we are receiving from our farmers.

Bodega Cocktail

2 oz. Licor 43
2 wedges lemons
Garnish:
1 lemon wedge

¾ oz. Wild Turkey
2 orange ½ wheels

1 orange ½ wheel

Directions

In a mixing glass, muddle the lemon wedges and orange half wheels. Add the Licor 43 and Wild Turkey, then top with ice. Shake in a tin for at least 30 seconds, then strain into a chilled cocktail glass. Garnish with lemon and orange. Enjoy!

Between Silk Sheets

1 oz. Cointreau
1 oz. Metaxa 5 Star Greek Brandy

1 oz. Benedictine & Brandy
½ oz. fresh lemon juice

Directions

Mix all ingredients in mixing glass or tin. Add ice and shake for 15 to 20 seconds. Strain into a chilled cocktail glass. Flamed orange twist garnish.

Submitted by Ted Kilgore, bar manager

BUZZARD'S BAR

Big Cedar Lodge Resort
612 Devil's Pool Rd.
Ridgedale, MO 65739
(417) 335-2777
www.big-cedar.com

You'll find a warm welcome at Buzzard's Bar. Legend and superstition were instrumental in naming this comfortable retreat, and while we don't expect you to find any live buzzards lurking in the shadows, you certainly will find an excellent selection of specialty drinks. There's comfortable seating indoors amid antique appointments and the usual collection of furred and feathered friends, or you may choose an outdoor setting on our patio or overlooking the pool. The Buzzard Bar features nightly entertainment at 8:30 p.m.

Buzzard's Brew
(This is one of the house favorites)

Strawberries
Chambord Liqueur

Vanilla ice cream

Directions

Mix all ingredients in a blender until smooth and creamy. Garnish with a fresh strawberry. Enjoy!

Submitted by Todd Leonard, asst. food and beverage director

CLASSIC SPORTS CAFE

Inside the Clarion Hotel
3333 S. Glenstone
Springfield, MO 65804
417-883-6550

Classic's Sports Café located in the Clarion Hotel is one of Springfield's Best Sports Bar & Grille. Offering over 20 TV's, you will have no problem finding your favorite game. A great menu featuring appetizers, sandwiches, steaks and our Award Winning Barbecue. The fun, casual atmosphere provides a great setting for Alumni Watch Parties, Social Clubs and Birthday Parties.

White Cosmopolitan

1½ oz. vodka
White cranberry juice

½ oz. Triple sec
Grenadine

Directions

Mix ingredients into shaker Shake until outside of shaker is very cold or frosted. Pour into martini glass.

*Pour a few drops of grenadine directly in the glass after you have poured the drink. Garnish with a lime twist.

Submitted by Michael DeForest

ST. JAMES WINES
PERFECT WITH EVERY MEAL.

"Award-Winning Wines
— from —
AMERICA'S MIDWEST WINERY™"

ST. JAMES WINERY

540 Sidney Street • St. James, Missouri
Conveniently located off I-44
7 Miles East of Rolla • Exit 195

stjameswinery.com • 800-280-9463

• Waldorf Chicken Salad • New England Clam Chowder • Bruschetta • Teriyaki Chicken •

Shrimp Louis • Alaskan Crab Salad • Shrimp Chowder • Spicy Chicken Wings • Oysters on the Half Shell • Gazpacho • Moussaka • Ratatouille

• Pear and Tuna Salad • Greek-Style Chicken • Sausage and Pasta • Meatloaf • Lasagna •

EMACK & BOLIO'S

216 E. Walnut St
Springfield, MO 65806
(417) 831-6336
www.emacksdowntown.com

Award-winning Boston ice cream. Smoothies, coffee, espresso, homemade soups, sandwiches and salads. All breads, pastries, and desserts are made from scratch. Fresh squeezed juices and smoothies come with vitamins, power boosters and energy shots while the cold creamy stuff comes in funky flavors like Grasshopper Pie and Twisted Dee-Light.

Frozen Mochachino

1 small scoop of Java (coffee) ice cream
1 shot of espresso
1 pump of coffee syrup

¼ scoop of ice
6 oz. of milk

Directions

Combine all ingredients. Blend until smooth and serve.

Submitted by Steve Bingham, owner

FOX AND HOUND

2035 E. Independence
(Next to Super WalMart)
Springfield, MO 65804
(417) 890-6289

Fox and Hound Pub and Grille provides a social gathering place offering high quality food, drinks and entertainment in an upscale, casual environment. We have 36 draft beers, over 60 bottled beers, a fully stocked bar and games galore. Come and see us for all of your sporting events on our 32 TVs.

Pineapple Upside Down Cake
You'll flip for this mix

1¼ oz. Malibu Coconut Rum
1 oz. pineapple juice

¾ oz. banana liqueur

Pour ingredients over ice in shaker, shake until chilled then pour into a martini glass. Splash of Grenadine on top (makes it look like a cherry).

Carribean Tea
You'll dream of the islands when you experience this.

1½ oz. Malibu Coconut Rum
1 oz. pineapple juice
1 oz. sweet and sour

¾ oz. banana liqueur
1 oz. orange juice

Mix ingredients in a shaker. Pour over ice in a tall tea glass. Top with a splash of Sprite. Garnish with an orange wedge.

Captain Con Leché
Kick up your heels with the Captain!

¾ oz. Captain Morgan Spice Rum
½ oz. Butterscotch schnapps

¾ oz. Kahlua coffee liqueur
3 oz. half & half

Mix ingredients in a shaker. Pour over ice in a tall tea glass. Top with a splash of Coke. Garnish with a cherry.

Submitted by Emily Eichelkraut, manager

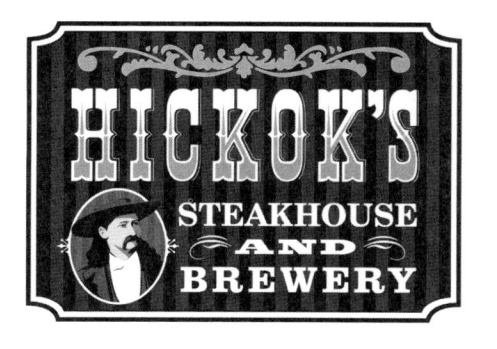

314 S. Patton
Springfield, MO 65804
(417) 872-1141
www.hickokssteakhouse.com

Family friendly, fun, and Affordable. The newest steakhouse in town. Hickok's Steakhouse and Brewery. Come visit the old west in one of the oldest buildings in downtown Springfield only a block from where the famous gunfight between Wild Bill Hickok and Dave Tutt happened in 1865. The first fast draw gunfight in America. Great Food, Great Beer, Great Fun, Lunch or Dinner Monday through Saturday. All at a Great Price. Hickok's Steakhouse and Brewery.

Cowboy Cosmo

2 oz. Applejack
¼ oz. Rose's lime juice
Round slice of orange peel

½ oz. Cointreau
¼ oz. cranberry juice

Directions

Combine all ingredients except orange peel in a shaker glass with ice. Shake well and strain into a chilled cocktail glass. Squeeze orange peel and drop in glass.

Pale Rider

1½ oz. Absolut Kurant vodka
2 oz. cranberry juice
1 oz. fresh lime juice
Lime wheel

½ oz. Peach Schnapps
1 oz. pineapple juice
¾ oz. simple syrup
Orange wheel

Directions

Build over ice in a pint glass. Roll back and forth into another pint glass to mix. Garnish with lime and orange wheels.

Submitted by Ted Kilgore, bar consultant

JEREMIAH'S NIGHT CLUB

2325 Bittersweet
(7 mm by water)
Lake Ozark, MO 65049
(573) 365-5500

Jeremiah's Nightclub, located on the second level of The Horny Toad entertainment complex, features state-of-the-art lighting and sound technology with 2 VIP seating areas and 2 bars. The outer expansive balcony includes a Tiki Bar and a 20 x 30 foot high definition projection TV.

A Passionate Rush

1½ oz. Ketel One Vodka
Pulp of 1 passion fruit

½ oz. Cointreau
Slice pineapple

Directions

Combine ingredients (except for pineapple) in an ice-filled shaker, shake to combine and chill. Strain mixture into chilled martini glass and garnish with pineapple slice.

Submitted by Shawn Rush, bar manager

McGUFFEY'S RESTAURANT & BAR

2600 W. Hwy. 76
Branson, MO 65616
(417) 336-3600
www.mcguffeys.com

Made with the orange flavored drink used by American astronauts in space, our signature specialty frozen adult beverage will be sure to send you into orbit! A drink found only at McGuffey's is represented by a half ton orange gorilla found in front of our restaurant for all driving Branson's famous "strip" to see. Come to McGuffey's and "Do the Wild Tang"!

O'Rang A Tang

½ c. Tang powdered orange drink mix
2 oz. Vodka
Ice, approx. 7 cups

2 oz. Triple Sec
1 oz. Everclear (100 proof grain alcohol)

Directions

Place Tang powder in the blender with about 5 cups of ice. Add the liquor & blend until smooth, adding additional ice as needed to make a slushy consistency. Pour into frosted mugs & garnish with orange slice if desired. Makes 4 ten oz. servings.

Submitted by Paul Militello, GM

PECKERS GOURMET GRILL & BAR

Gourmet Grill & Bar

3285 Bagnell Dam Blvd.
Lake Ozark, MO 65049
(573) 365-4085

Peckers Gourmet Grill & Bar has a fun family atmosphere, game room, and big screen for all your favorite sports. Breakfast served Saturday and Sunday. The Best Happy Hour at the Lake of the Ozarks.

Peckerita

2 oz. tequila
½ oz. triplesec
3 oz. cranberry juice

½ oz. razzmatazz
½ oz. lime juice

Directions

In a bar shaker over ice, add tequila, razzmatazz, triplesec, lime juice and cranberry juice. Serve in a margarita glass rimmed in your choice of salt or sugar on the rocks.

Submitted by Peckers bar staff

319 W. Walnut
Downtown" Springfield, MO
(417) 831-7221

Rasta Grill has been a staple of "Downtown" Springfield for close to 10 years. What started out as a 20 seat diner has grown into a 200 seat, full service restaurant. Our full menu of chicken, seafood, steaks, pastas and many other "fusion" dishes, coupled with a large selection of beer, wine and liquor, are offered for a quick lunch or a nice dinner with the family. We look forward to serving Springfield for another 10 years.

Rastapolitan

2 oz. Parrot Bay Pineapple Rum
2 oz. Cointreau
Splash of cranberry juice

2 oz. Bacardi Coconut Rum
Pineapple juice

Directions

Combine all the ingredients. Shake and serve in a chilled martini glass. Garnish with a slice of orange and a cherry.

Submitted by Mark Cotner, owner

Welcome to Central Missouri's
Lake of the Ozarks

The Original Floating Restaurant

4877 Highway 54
Osage Beach, MO 65065
(573) 348-2259

The Topsider is a top 40 dance club located at the Grand Glaize Bridge in Osage Beach, Mo. at the Lake of the Ozarks. It was conceived in an effort to establish a business on shore with a season longer than 100 days. It was built in 1981 for approximately 50 people. As business changed, we had to expand. We now have a complex that includes multi-level decks, a swimming pool, a tiki bar, a floating boat drive-in and the night club. We learned early on to market our specialty drinks. One of our most popular drinks is the Ha Ha Tonka Zonka.

Ha Ha Tonka Zonka

¾ oz. vodka
¾ oz. SoCo (Southern Comfort)

¾ oz. amaretto
¾ oz. Sloe Gin

Directions

Fill with pineapple juice. Shake, pour and enjoy!

Submitted by Kym Ebling, owner

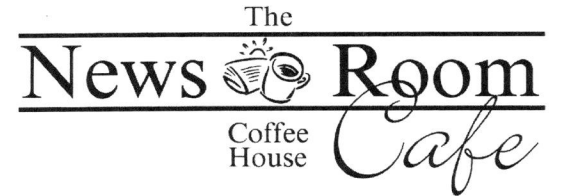

Inside the Clarion Hotel
3333 S. Glenstone
Springfield, MO 65804
417-883-6550

The NEWSROOM CAFE offers a wonderful breakfast buffet each morning and is the perfect place to have a morning coffee and catch up on the morning's headlines with your complimentary USA Today or the Wall Street Journal.

Clarion Coffee

⅛ oz. Bailey's Irish Cream
⅛ oz. Grand Marnier
Whipped cream

⅛ oz. Kaluha
Fresh hot coffee

Directions

In a clear glass coffee cup, pour in Kaluha, Grand Marnier and Bailey's Irish Cream. Fill cup to top with coffee, garnish with whipped cream and a chocolate cigarette.

Submitted by Michael DeForest

1620 E. Republic Rd.
Springfield, MO
(417) 823-8383

Touch is a beautiful restaurant with an American menu and a touch of Mediterranean. Belly dancing is featured on Thursday, Friday and Saturday nights. Featured entrees are Sea bass and Halibut. Desserts include chocolate torte and Bailey's Irish Cream Cheesecake.

Pomegranate Margarita

2 oz. Pomegranate juice
3½ oz. Sweet & Sour

1½ Tequila
1 oz. Triple-Sec

209 E. Walnut St.
Springfield, MO 65806
(417) 831-1480

Bijan's has been open for 9 years. It offers an exhibition kitchen and a martini lounge with a walk in cigar humidor. Bijan's has consistently won awards such as Best Restaurant, Best Service and Best Wine List.

Romeo & Julieta

4 oz. Captain Morgan Spiced Rum
3 oz. Chambord

1 oz. B&B
Squeeze of lemon and lime

Both submitted by Mike Jalili, owner

Index

MISCELLANEOUS

DESSERTS

BEVERAGES

An Adventure In
HEMINGWAY'S
BLUE WATER CAFE ®

Dining, Banquets, & Catering

DINE IN SPRINGFIELD'S MOST UNIQUE ATMOSPHERE!

Begin your adventure with Hemingway's famous Seafood Nachos or dive right into our Montego Bay Salad topped with Coconut Chicken. Creamy Alfredo Pasta, juicy Charbroiled Burgers, and Bonefish Willie's Fried Catfish Sandwich will all entice you to join us for lunch. Smoked Double Pork Chops, Crab Legs & Roasted Prime Rib, Shrimp Scampi, and Caribbean Chicken will be some of your favorites for dinner.
From our light and tasty Chicken Caesar Sandwich to the hearty 12-oz. center-cut Kansas City Strip Steak –your adventure in dining begins at Hemingway's!

Average Price Range … $5.29–$14.89

BREAKFAST BUFFET

7 a.m.–10 a.m. Monday–Saturday

Enjoy Scrambled Eggs, Bacon, Ham, Sausage, Breakfast Potatoes, Fried Catfish, Biscuits and Gravy, French Toast, Pancakes, Fresh-Baked Muffins and Pastries, and Fresh Fruit.

Adult.....$5.89   Children 5–10 years old....$2.29   Children 4 and younger....FREE
Complimentary orange juice with breakfast buffet!

LUNCH BUFFET

11 a.m.–2:30 p.m. Monday–Saturday

Hearty Sportsman's Buffet & Salad Bar—Help yourself to all you can eat.
Enjoy a bountiful Salad Bar, New England Clam Chowder, Carved Roast Beef, Ham or Turkey, Fried Catfish, Hot Entrée of the Day, Pasta with Marinara or Alfredo Sauce, Vegetables, Freshly Prepared Salads, Fresh-Baked Muffins, Cornbread, Cobbler, Bread Pudding, and much more!

Adult.....$8.29   Children 5–10 years old....$3.29   Children 4 and younger....FREE
Soup & Salad only......$7.89

DINNER BUFFET

5 p.m.–9 p.m. Monday–Saturday

Featuring: Crab Legs, Crayfish, Fried Shrimp, BBQ Ribs, Hot Entrée of the Day, Carved Roast Beef and Ham, Pasta with Marinara or Alfredo Sauce, New England Clam Chowder, Steamed Vegetables, Garden-Fresh Salad Bar, Seafood Pasta Salad, Fresh-Baked Cobbler, Chocolate Mousse, and Bread Pudding, just to name a few.

Adult.....$17.79   Children 5–10 years old....$6.79   Children 4 and younger....FREE

SUNDAY BRUNCH

9 a.m.–3 p.m. Sunday

Sunday Brunch is a culinary masterpiece featuring Carved Roast Beef and Ham, Made-to-Order Omelettes, Belgian Waffles with Strawberry Topping and Whipped Cream, Fluffy Scrambled Eggs, Sausage, Biscuits and Gravy, Chef's Entrées of the Day, Fresh Fruit, Garden Fresh Salad Bar, and Hemingway's Magnificent Dessert Bar with Fresh Baked Cakes, Cookies, Pastries, Creamy Key Lime Pie, and much more.

Adult.....$12.99   Children 5–10 years old....$3.99

Children 4 and younger....FREE
Items & prices subject to change.

Located on the fourth floor of
Bass Pro Shops® Outdoor World®,
1935 S. Campbell, Springfield, MO
(417) 891-5100

BP316614